Discover JOHN
THE LAMB OF GOD

by
Brent and Diane Averill

FAITH
ALIVE®
Christian Resources

Grand Rapids, Michigan

Cover photo: Corbis

The authors wish to acknowledge with thanks that in preparing their
manuscript for this study they drew on some ideas for discussion questions
and responses from two earlier studies produced in the Discover Your Bible
series: *Discover Jesus in John: Who He Is* (1992) and *Discover Jesus in John: Why
He Came* (1993) by Sylvia Boomsma. All rights reserved by Faith Alive
Christian Resources.

We welcome your comments. Call us at 1-800-333-8300 or e-mail us at
editors@faithaliveresources.org.

ISBN 978-1-59255-226-9

10 9 8 7 6 5 4 3 2

Contents

To the Leader

Prepare the Lesson

This leader guide is meant to assist you as a small group leader but not to substitute for your own work. As you prepare to lead each lesson, work first through the questions in the study guide. Then use the leader material to enrich your understanding of the passage. Prepare thoroughly before leading each group session so that you can lead without frequent references to notes. This approach will free you to concentrate on leadership responsibilities, keep eye contact with group members, and listen carefully.

Get Ready to Lead

Learn to think in terms of questions. As you prepare to lead a lesson, ask yourself questions and try to discover the answers yourself. This will prepare you to anticipate group members' questions and thus help others discover truths from God's Word.

Lead with Questions

Use questions to direct the group discussion. Draw out positive contributions by asking questions. Break down difficult or unclear questions into smaller, concise ones. Also use questions to respond to wrong or problematic answers. If you learn to lead others to truth by questions, you will be a good Bible discovery leader. The questions in this study are designed to be used with the New International Version of the Bible, but other translations can also be used.

Help to Apply

Gently help group members discover the meaning of God's message for their own lives. Be careful not to be judgmental of persons who may not yet seem to be applying the truths you encounter together. It's the Spirit's work to apply God's Word to people's hearts. Tactfully let the group know how the Spirit is applying the Word in your own heart and life. Pray faithfully for the Spirit's work in others.

While giving people the time and space to apply biblical truths as the Spirit leads them, simply try to help group members see that there is a relationship between the Bible and life. Questions for reflection at the end of each session invite everyone to take time for personal reflection and optional sharing. Try to offer at least a few minutes for reflection time toward the end of each lesson, and encourage group members to do follow-up reflection at home.

Leadership Training

If more than one group in your setting is using this Bible study, we strongly encourage leaders to meet regularly for discussion of the lessons, for prayer, and for mutual support. If this study is being used in a Coffee Break Small Groups program, each leader should have a copy of the *Coffee Break Evangelism Manual with Director's Handbook*. This book is a basic "how-to" guide for establishing and leading a Bible discovery group. Reread the book or portions of it periodically and review it at the beginning of each season.

Leaders will also find it helpful to attend one or more of the many leadership training workshops offered each year in connection with small group ministry.

For more information,

- call toll-free 1-888-644-0814, e-mail smallgroups@crcna.org, or visit www.FaithAliveResources.org/DYB (for training advice and general information)

- call toll-free 1-800-333-8300 or visit www.FaithAliveResources.org (to order materials)

Introduction

The last days of Jesus' life have inspired countless books, movies, and musical pieces, and students of the Bible quickly discover that the events of those days fill the entire second half of the book of John. Shortly after raising his friend Lazarus from the dead at Bethany (John 11), Jesus rides into Jerusalem as the promised Son of David, the Messiah, the Son of God (John 12)—setting in motion an amazing week of events that complete his mission to save us from sin and death forever.

The gospel ("good news") message is true! Jesus Christ is "the Lamb of God, who takes away the sin of the world" (John 1:29). He became the ultimate sacrifice for sin by dying on a cross for our sake, and he conquered death and rose to life again so that "whoever believes in him shall not perish but have eternal life" (3:16).

As this study continues into the second half of the gospel account written by John, we pray that it may draw you closer to the one and only Savior, the eternal Son of God who "became flesh" to show us "the full extent of his love" (1:14; 13:1).

While many people can learn to read commentaries and gain understanding about the gospel, it takes the power of the Holy Spirit to change people through the gospel message. Some members of your group may have read and studied John before. Others may be looking at John for the first time. Some may not question anything about this Bible book, such as its authorship or the content of the miracles it records. Others, influenced by the skepticism of our age, may question every claim they encounter. They might view Christianity as just one choice among many valid religions.

Just as John wrote this gospel account in the cultural context of his day, we should aim to bring its message into our culture. Be prepared for the skeptic who not only needs to hear the truth but also needs to sense the love of Christ. Pray for wisdom to answer skeptical questions in a way that does not compromise the Word of God but also communicates in a loving, respectful way (Eph. 4:15; 1 Pet. 3:15-16). Ask the Holy Spirit for wisdom to discern questions that come not only from the head but also from the heart.

Some of the lessons in this study cover a bit more material than others. As you work through these lessons with your group, remember that you do not have to cover each passage in an exhaustive way. Make use of the Scriptures and the questions in this study to whet people's appetites for spiritual growth and learning, and encourage everyone to keep studying on their own.

Glossary of Terms

Abraham—the father of the Israelite nation whom God called to follow him in faith. God also promised to bless "all peoples on earth" through Abraham (Gen. 12:3). Jesus ultimately fulfilled that promise by making God's salvation possible for people of all nations. Abraham is also called the father of all believers (Rom. 4:11-12; see Gal. 3:29).

Aramaic—one of the common languages used in Palestine during the time of Jesus' public ministry.

baptism—In the ministry of John the Baptist, this was an outward sign indicating repentance on the part of the sinner who wanted to be forgiven (Mark 1:4; Acts 19:1-5). Baptism in Christ is a sign of the inward washing away of sin and the dying of the sinful nature to rebirth and renewal (Acts 22:16; Rom. 6:1-4; Titus 3:4). This sacrament is usually performed by sprinkling with or by immersion in water.

blasphemy—scoffing at or misusing the name of God. The Jewish leaders accused Jesus of blasphemy because he claimed to be God, and they refused to believe him.

the Christ—see **Messiah**.

David—a shepherd boy from Bethlehem who became one of the greatest kings of ancient Israel. He wrote many psalms and established the worship of God in Jerusalem. (See 1 Sam. 16:1-1 Kings 2:12.) According to God's promise in 2 Samuel 7, the Messiah would be a descendant of David.

eternal life—life that lasts forever with God. It begins when one receives Jesus by faith as Savior, and it reaches fulfillment in the new heaven and earth when the believer's soul is reunited with his or her resurrected body to live in God's presence forever (1 Cor. 15:20-54).

the Father—the first person of the Trinity. The other two persons are God the Son (Jesus Christ) and God the Holy Spirit. They are three persons in one being.

Feast of Dedication—a winter celebration commemorating the rededication of the Jewish temple in Jerusalem after a defeat of Greek oppressors in 164 B.C. This feast is also known as Hanukkah or the Festival of Lights.

Feast of Tabernacles—a fall harvest festival commemorating God's covenant with Israel during their stay in the wilderness after being freed from slavery in Egypt. This was one of three annual feasts that all Jewish males were required to attend; the other two were the Feast of Passover and the Feast of Weeks (Pentecost).

Galilee—the northernmost province of ancient Palestine. It was separated from Judea by Samaria, and the Aramaic dialect of this region was noticeably different from the Aramaic spoken in Judea. It was also an area where many Gentiles lived. Most Jews in the south thought Galilee was on the fringe of Judaism, both culturally and spiritually. Jesus grew up in the village of Nazareth in Galilee, and a great deal of his public ministry took place in this region.

glory—splendor, majesty, power, worth, excellence of quality and character. Jesus revealed God's glory and his unity with God through his teaching and miracles (John 2:11) and through his death and resurrection.

gospel—This word literally means "good news" and refers to the message of God's salvation from sin and the promise of eternal life through Jesus Christ. This word can also refer to one of the first four books of the New Testament (Matthew, Mark, Luke, and John) that tell the good news story about Jesus.

grace—God's undeserved favor and forgiving love. Jesus is the full expression of God's grace "in the flesh" for the salvation of all who believe in him as Lord and Savior.

Greeks—another name for Gentiles who lived in Israel and who mainly spoke Greek as a result of Greek influence over the region since the time of Alexander the Great (331 B.C.).

Holy Spirit—the third person of the Trinity. The other two persons are God the Father and God the Son (Jesus Christ). They are three persons in one being.

Isaiah—one of the major prophets of Israel. Isaiah prophesied from 740-681 B.C. and delivered a number of clear prophecies about the Messiah of Israel.

Jacob—grandson of Abraham and father of the twelve tribes of Israel. God renamed him Israel, which means "he struggles with God" (see Gen. 32:28). Jacob bought some land near Sychar and dug a well there (John 4:5-6). The land was given to the descendants of Jacob's son Joseph, and in Jesus' day this well was in Samaritan territory.

Jerusalem—the capital of Judea and the religious center for all Jews. The temple was located there.

Jewish ruling council—see **Sanhedrin.**

Jews—descendants of the Israelite tribes of (mainly) Judah and Benjamin who returned from exile in Babylon to rebuild Jerusalem and the temple of the Lord after 538 B.C. The gospel writer John uses this term frequently, sometimes to refer to the Jewish people but most often to refer to the Jewish religious leaders in Jerusalem.

John the Baptist—the last prophet who called people to repentance to help them prepare for the coming of the Messiah. John baptized people in the Jordan River as a symbol of their repentance and preparation. John was also Jesus' cousin. (See Luke 1:5-66; 3:1-6, 15-20.)

John the disciple—a close friend and disciple of Jesus who wrote the gospel of John. He also wrote three letters and the book of Revelation in the New Testament.

Lamb of God—John the Baptist used this phrase to describe Jesus at the time of his baptism as he began his public ministry (John 1:29, 35). This title implied that Jesus as Messiah would be a sacrificial substitute for sins (based on traditional sacrifices for Passover and atonement for sin—see Ex. 12; Lev. 16; see also Heb. 10:1-18).

the Law (and the Prophets)—In Jesus' day people often used this term to refer to the body of Old Testament writings that made up the Jewish Scriptures (see Matt. 5:17; 22:40).

manna—a food that God provided for the Israelites during their travels in the desert after their release from slavery in Egypt. The manna appeared on the ground each morning, except on the Sabbath, and could be used for baking bread. Many of the Jews believed the Messiah would renew the sending of this "bread from heaven" (see John 6:32-35).

Messiah—the promised deliverer of God's people. Both the Hebrew word *Messiah* and the Greek word *Christ* mean "Anointed One." Through the prophets God promised to send the Messiah to deliver God's people from evil oppressors and to rule them in righteousness forever. The people misunderstood these promises, however, and looked for a Messiah who would be a political ruler and gather an army to rout all their physical enemies. But as Jesus revealed through his work and teaching, the Messiah came to save God's people from the oppression of sin and death and to give them new life forever with God. He rules today in heaven at the right hand of the Father, and when he comes again at the end of time he will fully establish God's everlasting kingdom of righteousness on earth. (See Matt. 26:63-64; John 16:5-16; 1 Cor. 15; Rev. 21:1-5; 22:1-5.)

money changers—officials who exchanged Roman currency into the Jewish currency acceptable to temple authorities for the payment of offerings and temple taxes.

Moses—the leader of the Israelites when God delivered them from slavery in Egypt and as they lived in the wilderness before entering the promised land (Palestine). Moses received the law from God and taught it to the Israelites.

Passover—This feast took place each spring to celebrate the Israelites' exodus from slavery in Egypt. The name commemorates God's protection of Israelite households during a final plague sent to convince the Egyptian king (pharaoh) to let the Israelites go. God promised that upon seeing the blood of a sacrificed lamb on the doorframes of a house, God would *pass over* that house and not allow the plague of death to take the life of the firstborn in that house (see Ex. 12).

Pharisees—an elite group that emphasized precise obedience to scriptural and traditional law. A number of Pharisees were part of the Sanhedrin (the Jewish ruling council).

priests—officials who served in the temple and belonged to the tribe of Levi; also often called Levites.

Pool of Siloam—a pool at the southern end of Jerusalem.

the Prophet—In Deuteronomy 18:15-19 Moses describes this person whom God promised to raise up to teach the people in the name of the Lord. While other great prophets such as Elijah, Isaiah, Jeremiah, and John the Baptist served God faithfully and filled this description in some ways, Jesus is the ultimate fulfillment of this promise.

rabbi—a Jewish religious scholar and teacher. Well-known rabbis often had disciples.

Sabbath—the seventh day of the week (Saturday), set aside as a day of rest and restoration according to the law of Moses. Jewish religious leaders developed a stringent code of rules for keeping the Sabbath, and Jesus often criticized them for being too legalistic in this regard (see Mark 2:23-3:6; Luke 13:10-17; John 5:16-17; 7:21-24).

Samaritans—residents of Samaria who descended from the ten northern tribes of Israel. The Samaritans had intermarried with other peoples in the region and claimed that God was to be worshiped at Mount Gerizim, not in Jerusalem. They despised the Jews (who descended from the two southern tribes of Judah and Benjamin), and the Jews despised them.

Sanhedrin—the ruling council of the Jews, made up of seventy-one officials including Pharisees, Sadducees, leading elders, legal experts, and priests. Nicodemus was a member of this group (John 3:1), and so was Joseph of Arimathea (Mark 15:43; John 19:38-42).

Satan—this name means "accuser" (see Zech. 3:1) and refers to the fallen angel who tempted humanity to sin and wants to destroy God's kingdom. The Bible refers to this being as "the evil one" (Matt. 6:13); "a roaring lion looking for someone to devour" (1 Pet. 5:8); "the great dragon . . . that ancient serpent called the devil, Satan, who leads the whole world astray" (Rev. 12:9); "the prince of this world" who "now stands condemned" (John 16:11); and more. When Jesus conquered sin and death for our sake, he dealt Satan a fatal blow (see Gen. 3:14-15) and destroyed Satan's power to accuse us of our sins before God (Col. 2:13-15). At the end of time, Jesus will completely defeat Satan (Rev. 20:7-10). Though Satan is still powerful and dangerous today, he cannot snatch us from God's hand (John 10:27-30).

Sea of Galilee—a large freshwater lake in Galilee that was also known as the Sea of Tiberias (after a town on its western coast, named for a Roman caesar—see John 6:1, 23; 21:1).

Son of God—Jesus used this term to describe his relationship as God the Son with God the Father. The Jewish leaders clearly understood this term to mean having equality with God.

Son of Man—Jesus used this term to describe his humanity as well as to refer to a title associated with the Messiah as described by the prophet Daniel (see Dan. 7:13-14; Matt. 24:30; 25:31; 26:64).

Spirit—see **Holy Spirit**.

synagogue—the local gathering place for weekly services in Jewish communities. There were many synagogues throughout Palestine, but the only temple was in Jerusalem.

temple—the religious center of Judaism in the Old Testament and in Jesus' day. Located in Jerusalem, it was the place of worship and sacrifice, the site of major Jewish festivals, and the gathering place of religious thinkers, teachers, and leaders.

the Twelve—another name for Jesus' twelve disciples.

the Word—In the original Greek language of John's text, the word *logos* (translated as "Word") could have several meanings. Greek philosophers often used this word to refer to the unifying force of the universe. Given the context of statements like "In him all things were made" and "In him was life" (John 1:3-4), we can see that John was using *logos* to speak of Jesus as the divine Word who holds all things together (see also Col. 1:15 20).

Lesson 1
John 11

From Death to Life—for God's Glory

Additional Related Scriptures

Psalm 66:18
Matthew 26:3-5
Luke 7:11-17; 8:51-56; 10:38-39;
    11:9-13

John 1:1-2, 5, 10-12, 16-18, 29; 3:16,
    19-21; 4:34; 5:16, 18, 21-29; 6:38,
    40-42, 54, 66; 7:1, 27, 30-32, 45, 52;
    8:12, 23-27, 47-59; 9:4-5, 31, 39;
    10:22-33, 39, 40-42; 20:24-28

Introductory Notes

Many people assume that if only they could witness a miracle from God, they would believe in God. But as this lesson shows, many skeptics refused to believe in Jesus as God even though he brought a dead man back to life.

John 11 describes one of the most amazing miracles of Jesus: he raised his friend Lazarus from the grave although he had been dead for four days. In this episode we also see Jesus "deeply moved . . . and troubled" in spirit, so affected by the death of his friend that he wept openly (John 11:33, 35).

The Son of God cares so deeply for us that he came to conquer death for our sake and offer us full life with God forever. As you study this lesson together, ask God for the wisdom to share with others how this offer from God still stands.

As you will notice, the material for this lesson is lengthy and includes references to many Scripture passages, most of which are from earlier chapters in the book of John. At various points this lesson aims to review the main teachings John has presented about Jesus so that group members can see how integrally this episode fits into the whole of Jesus' mission. If your group is beginning this study soon after finishing Part One of *Discover John,* you'll be able to move quickly through the review material. If you studied Part One several months ago, you may want to look back at various key passages on the purpose of Jesus' coming and the ways people reacted to him. If your group is beginning Part Two without having studied Part One, you may want to review John 1-10 and summarize its main points before discussing John 11 together. The Scripture passages listed in this lesson will help you locate the teachings in John 1-10 that pertain to the discussion of John 11.

Optional Share Question

Note: The optional share question in each lesson may serve well at the beginning of your session or at some other time during your discussion. Use or adapt each share question in a way that works best for your group. (If you have a copy of the *NIV Serendipity Bible for Groups,* you may find that some of the share questions it offers can also enhance your group discussions.)

Describe a deeply emotional funeral you have attended. What made it emotional?

1. *John 11:1-6*

Note: You may want to read or review together the full narrative of the death and resurrection of Lazarus (John 11:1-44) before discussing the following questions. Some details mentioned later in the story shed light on events described at the beginning. In addition, a review of John 10:40-42 can help recall the setting in which part of the story takes place.

a. What do we learn about Mary, Martha, and Lazarus? Describe their relationship to Jesus.

Mary, her sister Martha, and their brother Lazarus lived in Bethany, a village about two miles from Jerusalem. From the gospel of Luke we know that Jesus and his disciples became close friends with this family, sometimes using their home as a place of rest during their travels in ministry (Luke 10:38-39). Mary is further identified as the woman who "poured perfume on the Lord and wiped his feet with her hair" (John 11:2), an episode covered in John 12. Lazarus, who "now lay sick" (11:2), is mentioned only in the gospel of John, and his sisters describe him as one whom Jesus loves.

• **What does it mean that Jesus loved Mary, Martha, and Lazarus?**

The Greek word describing Jesus' love for Lazarus in John 11:3 is *phileo,* referring to brotherly love, and the word describing his love for Mary, Martha, and Lazarus in 11:5 is *agape,* referring to unconditional love. As God, Jesus loves all people unconditionally, but now that he is also human, it can be said that he loves people as brothers, sisters, and "friends" (*philos*— 15:15), "children of God" welcomed into the family of God (1:12; Eph. 2:19; 1 John 3:1).

• **Is it surprising that Jesus had close friends? Why or why not?**

b. What message did the sisters send to Jesus, and what was his response?

Mary and Martha sent word that Lazarus was ill, implying that they needed Jesus to come and heal him as soon as possible.

- **Why do you think Jesus said this sickness would not end in death?**

- **What was the greater purpose for which this sickness occurred?**

From later details in the story we can see that Jesus knew Lazarus was severely ill and would die. In fact, Lazarus may well have died by the time Jesus received the sisters' message (see John 11:14). But Jesus pointed beyond his friend's death to predict a resurrection miracle, knowing that this was "for God's glory" and that Jesus himself would be "glorified through it" (11:4).

- **What's surprising about Jesus' response?**

One would think that because Jesus was a good friend, he would go immediately to help Lazarus. But Jesus delayed going for two days.

- **Why would Jesus delay?**

Note: If group members are curious about this and you have enough time, you may want to explore the following discussion together, noting from the start that we cannot be certain why Jesus delayed going to Bethany.
John doesn't explain the reason for Jesus' delay, but it seems that somehow it had to do with the greater purpose of glorifying God (see also 11:15). Some interpreters have suggested that Jesus delayed because a miracle of resurrection would reveal Jesus more clearly as the Son of God than a miracle of healing would. But that kind of interpretation could mislead us to set God's desire for glory over against God's compassion and care for people. (In other words, it could lead us to ask, *Why would a caring, compassionate God put his people through such misery in order to reveal his glory?*) Besides, Jesus had brought others back to life before (Luke 7:11-17; 8:51-56), and Elijah and Elisha had long ago been given power to do the same (see 1 Kings 17:17-24; 2 Kings 4:17-37). So a resurrection miracle would not convince skeptics of Jesus' identity any more than a healing miracle would. If necessary, remind group members that miracles do not ultimately produce faith (see John 10:22-33 and a discussion of the purpose of miracles in lesson 6 of the leader guide for Part One of this study).
Other scholars have noted that several details in the story can help us piece together a more logical response. From John 11:14 we know that Jesus

knew before leaving for Bethany that Lazarus was dead. And from John 11:17 we learn that by the time Jesus arrived at Bethany, "Lazarus had already been in the tomb for four days." In addition, John 10:40 shows that Jesus was in the region across the Jordan River "where John [the Baptist] had been baptizing in the early days." This region was likely about 20 miles (32 km) from the town where Lazarus and his sisters lived (see 1:28), or about a day's journey (see map in study guide). So if the messenger's journey and Jesus' journey took about a day each, and if Jesus delayed for two days, Lazarus would have to have died soon after the messenger left Bethany—otherwise he couldn't have been "in the tomb for four days" (11:17). In other words, Jesus may have seen no urgency in going to heal Lazarus, because he likely knew Lazarus was already dead (see 11:14).

Though some group members may find this bit of detective work intriguing, others may rightly point out that it is speculative. Even if the details show that Lazarus probably died before the messenger reached Jesus, they don't explain why Jesus delayed for two days. Some scholars add that a popular superstition taught that the soul stayed around for three days after a person died, hoping to return to the body—so the fact that Lazarus had been dead for four days meant he was unquestionably dead. But that idea is also speculative.

From the larger context of the story we recall that the Jewish authorities in Jerusalem wanted to kill Jesus (5:16, 18; 7:1; 8:59). Jesus had left Judea after an encounter with some leaders who'd tried to stone him (10:31-40). John also reports that Jesus escaped from being arrested or killed on several other occasions because his time had "not yet come" (7:6, 30; 8:20). This means that God's appointed time for Jesus' death had not yet arrived. As we'll see in later passages (12:23, 27; 13:1; 17:1), the right time for Jesus' death was during the upcoming Passover feast, when Jesus was revealed as "the Lamb of God, who takes away the sin of the world" (1:29). So in light of this larger context we might say that Jesus delayed going to Bethany because the time wasn't right. But again an objector might say that this suggestion is speculative.

Whatever the case, Jesus' delay somehow points to the greater purpose of his mission, as implied in these statements: "This sickness . . . is for God's glory so that God's Son may be glorified through it" (11:4) and "For your sake I am glad I was not there, so that you may believe" (11:15).

- **Who else had an infirmity that was for a wider purpose?**

Recall together that in John 9 Jesus healed a man who was born blind "so that the work of God might be displayed in his life" (9:3). If you have time, review your discussion of that passage from lesson 11 in Part One of this study. As you discuss this matter, be sensitive to group members who may have difficulty accepting that God has full control over this world. One of the biggest barriers to faith is the problem of suffering and how a good God could allow it. Leave room for the Spirit to speak to everyone through the Scriptures, and be thoughtful and patient as ideas are discussed. There is much we do not understand about pain and suffering, but we do know that things do not happen outside the design of the loving God.

2. John 11:7-16

   a. Why didn't the disciples want Jesus to go back to Judea?

- **Why might they have been afraid?**

The disciples knew that the Jewish leaders were looking for a way to arrest and kill Jesus (see John 5:16, 18; 7:1, 32; 8:59; 10:31, 39). Even though Jesus had escaped from the religious leaders before, the disciples knew that those leaders would be watching for an opportunity to arrest Jesus and put an end to his ministry.

   b. How did Jesus answer them?

- **What did he mean by "twelve hours of daylight"?**

The New Bible Commentary explains, "The reference to a twelve-hour day is based on Jewish reckoning, which divided the period between sunrise and sunset into twelve equal parts. These parts varied in length according to the time of year."

- **What did Jesus mean when he talked about walking in daylight and stumbling around at night?**

Jesus' comments about day and night hours sound similar to earlier statements he made in John 9:4-5 in connection with being "the light of the world." Recall your discussion of that passage from Part One of this study, or summarize along these lines:

> Jesus was feeling an urgency to do as much as possible to complete his mission faithfully for God, just as diligent workers make the most of remaining daylight hours to finish their day's work. Jesus also seems to have been telling his disciples that now, while he was still with them as "the light of the world," they should make the most of learning from him and responding to him.

In other words, in John 11 Jesus was implying that the work God had called him to do was more important than avoiding threats and difficulties in and around Jerusalem.

- How did Jesus clear up the disciples' confusion about Lazarus?

When he said he had to go to Bethany to wake up Lazarus, Jesus meant he was going to raise Lazarus from the sleep of death. At first the disciples thought he was talking about natural sleep that would help Lazarus heal. So Jesus made clear that Lazarus had died and that God would use this event to help increase their faith.

c. *How did Thomas react?*

Thomas apparently understood that something important was going to happen, so he urged the disciples to follow Jesus even if that meant they would die with him.

- What tone of voice do you hear when you read Thomas's statement?

This question can help group members see that sometimes a statement can be read in different ways. In this case, if we are used to thinking of Thomas as a doubter (see 20:24-27), we might tend to read his statement here as a response of resignation and despair. But, as the *NIV Study Bible* reminds us, Thomas was also "capable of devotion and courage." (See also 20:28.)

3. *John 11:17-27*

a. *Describe the scene as Jesus arrived in Bethany.*

- Who came out to meet him?

Lazarus had been in the grave for four days, and many friends and acquaintances had gathered to comfort Mary and Martha. Martha went out to meet Jesus when she heard he was approaching Bethany. The short distance from Bethany to Jerusalem made it relatively easy for "many Jews [to] come to Martha and Mary to comfort them in the loss of their brother." John likely notes this short distance to remind readers that Jesus was now close to the city where many of his enemies were (see 11:7-8).

b. *What did Martha say to Jesus, and what did she mean?*

Martha's words show that she knew Jesus could make a sick person well. Though some commentators have read her opening words ("If you had been here") as a rebuke, she is probably simply expressing regret and grief that Jesus hadn't been available to heal Lazarus before he died.

17

- Why does she comment that God would give Jesus anything he asked?

It appears that Martha also knew Jesus could bring Lazarus back to life. She most likely had heard about others whom Jesus had raised (see Luke 7:11-17; 8:51-56). She also knew about Jesus' close connection with God (John 10:30) and was familiar with the teaching about God giving what is asked in line with his will (Luke 11:9-13; John 9:31).

c. *Did she understand Jesus' response about Lazarus rising again?*

Though she believed in "the resurrection at the last day" (John 11:24; see 5:24-29), it seems that Martha wasn't thinking Lazarus would return to life before then. But Jesus was making a greater claim than Martha understood.

- What "I am" statement does Jesus make here?

- What's the significance of these words?

It would be difficult to overstate the meaning of Jesus' claim "I am the resurrection and the life" (11:25). Jesus was saying he had power and authority over life and death. This was always known to be the domain of God (5:21), so again Jesus was clearly claiming to be God (see 5:24-27).
Note: If you haven't discussed Jesus' "I am" statements before, you may want to note that Jesus used this emphatic construction often in his teaching ministry. The expression clearly echoed the way God named himself when calling Moses to lead the Israelites out of Egypt (Ex. 3:14), so by using this phrase, Jesus was claiming to be God. We'll discuss this matter in more detail when we look at John 14.

- What did Jesus mean when he said that people who believe in him "will never die"?

Recall earlier discussions you may have had on this topic while doing Part One of this study (see John 3:16; 5:21-29). Jesus is referring to spiritual death here, and he makes it clear that people would continue to die physically until "the last day" (6:40, 54).

- Why did Jesus ask Martha, "Do you believe this?"

Jesus was not simply having a theological discussion with Martha. He was asking for a commitment of faith. She responded by saying she believed in him as the Messiah (Christ), the promised deliverer of God's people. Though she probably didn't understand everything he was saying about life and death, she knew by faith who he was.

5. **John 11:28-37**

  a. *What did Mary do when Martha said Jesus was asking for her?*

Mary got up immediately and went out to meet Jesus at the same place where Martha had met him.

- **How did Mary greet Jesus?**

Mary fell before Jesus' feet, showing deep respect, and then she said almost the same thing Martha had said to Jesus earlier: "Lord, if you had been here, my brother would not have died." She was weeping, and so were the mourners who had come with her.

  b. *How did Jesus react to the situation?*

Jesus was "deeply moved" by the emotion of Mary and the mourners, and he asked where the grave of Lazarus was. Then, when the people said, "Come and see, Lord," Jesus wept (11:34-35).

- **Given the fact that Jesus would soon raise Lazarus back to life, why was he so deeply moved and why did he weep?**

Commentators note that the Greek word for "deeply moved" suggests a "groaning in one's spirit" that can include a kind of indignation, or anger. In contrast, the word for "wept" (*dakryo*, "shed tears") denotes Jesus' quiet weeping as compared to Mary and the others' "weeping" (*klaio*), which literally means "wailing."

Some scholars have suggested that Jesus was overcome with compassionate emotion when he saw Mary and the others grieving. Other interpreters have suggested that Jesus became upset at the people's lack of understanding and trust in his ability to raise people from the dead. Still others suggest that his "groaning" or deep emotion was in response to death itself.

  c. *How did the mourners react to the fact that Jesus wept?*

They affirmed that Lazarus had been a dear friend of Jesus, and yet some of them stated that he should have been able to keep Lazarus from dying.

Point out that these responses show how easily people can jump to conclusions. While Jesus definitely was a close friend of Lazarus, that fact wasn't necessarily proved by his weeping. And although Jesus was the

Messiah who was also a friend of Lazarus, that didn't mean Jesus was obligated to keep Lazarus from dying. As Jesus often had to remind people, his mission was to do the will of the Father who sent him (John 4:34; 6:38).

6. **John 11:38-44**

   What happened at the tomb?

   - **What did the tomb look like?**

   - **How did Martha react to the idea of rolling the stone away?**

   - **How did Jesus respond to her concern?**

   The tomb was a cave with a stone laid in front of its entrance. Martha objected to opening the tomb because she knew that by now her brother's body would be giving off a terrible odor. Jesus gently responded by saying that if she believed, she would "see the glory of God" (11:40). In other words, she would see that Lazarus's sickness "would not end in death" but reveal God's glory (11:4). As Jesus had said earlier, "Your brother will rise again" (11:23).

   - **Why did Jesus pray aloud to God?**

   Jesus sometimes prayed aloud so that the people around him would benefit. He explained that he wanted the people there to realize that he always depended on the Father and that the Father had truly sent him to be the Messiah. Everything that Jesus did was in line with the Father's will, including the miracle that these people would soon see.

   - **What happened next?**

   In response to Jesus' call, Lazarus "came out" of the tomb, and Jesus told the people to unwrap him and "let him go." Lazarus was now freed from the imprisonment of the grave. Commentators add that the brief description of Lazarus's return to life shows, as in many other miracle stories, that the main point of the account is to reveal God's glory.

7. **John 11:45-57**

   Note: If you're running out of discussion time for this lesson, you might simply summarize this section of John 11 and ask group members if they have specific questions about it that they'd like to discuss. Then close by inviting everyone to focus on the questions for reflection at the end of the session and to ask God for guidance in finding answers throughout the coming week.

a. What were the people's reactions to the raising of Lazarus?

"Many of the Jews who had come to visit" the grieving sisters in Bethany "put their faith in" Jesus. Some, however, apparently with malicious intent, went to the religious leaders in Jerusalem to report "what Jesus had done."

- **How did the religious leaders respond to this news?**

They called for a meeting of the Sanhedrin, the Jewish ruling council.

- **What was their concern?**

It's surprising that instead of looking into what actually happened, the Jewish leaders were concerned that so many people were following Jesus. On the surface they gave the appearance of being concerned for the nation, but it's clear that they feared losing their political standing with the Roman authorities. As in several other episodes described earlier, the religious leaders didn't really deal with who Jesus was. Although they acknowledged his miraculous signs, they didn't want to follow him. In other words, they refused to believe he was the Messiah. Jesus didn't fit their idea of what the Messiah should be, so they rejected him (see John 5:16-18; 6:41-42, 52, 66; 7:27, 52; 8:23-27, 47-59; 10:22-33).

- **How do we react today when God doesn't fit into our plans?**

b. Did Caiaphas know what he was saying?

- **Did one man die for the people?**

Caiaphas was making a political calculation that Jesus was expendable and that it would be better for everyone if he were killed. Little did Caiaphas know, though, that he was also making a prophetic statement. Jesus had become human to die sacrificially for his people, which included not only the Jewish nation but also "the scattered children of God."

- **Who were these "scattered children"?**

Recall Jesus' comments about "other sheep" in John 10:16. Jesus was referring to Gentile believers, people from all other nations who would believe in him and be saved.

- **Who are God's scattered children today? Are they all from other nations, or do some live in our neighborhoods? In our own families? In our own groups of friends?**

c. *What did the Jewish leaders plan to do, and how did Jesus respond?*

The leaders began plotting to take Jesus' life. Although they'd tried to have Jesus arrested before and some of them had also tried to stone him (7:30, 32, 45; 8:59; 10:33, 39), the religious leaders now began planning a strategy to get rid of him. So they sent out the word that if anyone knew where Jesus was, that person "should report it" to them.

- **Where was Jesus?**

John reports that Jesus withdrew to a village called Ephraim in a region near the desert.

- **Why did Jesus go away?**

The *NIV Study Bible* offers this explanation: "Knowing the attitude of his opponents, he withdrew. He would die for others, but in his own time, not that of his enemies." As we learn in later chapters, God's appointed time for Jesus' death was during the great Passover feast. The religious leaders wouldn't like this, and they even tried to avoid killing him during the festivities to avoid a riot (Matt. 26:3-5)—but they couldn't force God's hand.

Questions for Reflection

What does the story of Lazarus teach us about death?

What does it teach about Jesus and who he is?

Think about sharing this story with someone you know who doesn't know Jesus. What would you say?

If you have time, use these questions to reflect together on the lesson material before closing your session. Invite group members to share what they have learned, and if they aren't sure they agree with everything covered, allow room for them to discuss their thoughts. If you're out of time, however, you could suggest that everyone reflect on these questions at home, ask God for guidance in responding to them, and bring their questions or comments to your next meeting.

Also remember to pray for your group members, asking the Spirit of God to speak to their hearts and to help each one grow through this continuing study of the book of John.

Lesson 2
John 12:1-19

Worship, Honor, and Unbelief

Additional Related Scriptures

Deuteronomy 15:11
Psalm 118:25-27
Zechariah 9:9-10
Matthew 21:1-11; 25:37-40
Mark 11:1-11

Luke 19:29-44; 24:27
John 11:47-48
Acts 1:6-9; 2:1-39
Philippians 2:9-11

Introductory Notes

People respond to the person of Jesus in many ways, and this lesson covers a range of those responses. The story about Mary anointing Jesus with oil stands out in Scripture as an extravagant act of devotion. She shows herself to be, as some would say, "sold out for Christ."

In this lesson we also see people who follow Jesus only when it suits their purpose. The crowds, for example, honor him gladly, thinking he will bring them physical or political relief. But as we will see in later lessons, these same crowds reject Jesus a few days later and call for his execution.

Lurking in the shadows are others who have never understood Jesus. Their own sinful choices make it impossible for them to understand the real message and mission of Jesus (John 3:16-21). As a result, they reject him and try to stop others from following him.

Optional Share Question

Can you think of a time when you were excessively grateful? Describe the circumstances.

1. *John 12:1-6*

   a. *Why is Jesus in Bethany, and what is he celebrating?*

   While traveling to Jerusalem to celebrate the Passover feast (as all Jewish men were required to do), Jesus has stopped in Bethany to see his friends, and they are giving a banquet in his honor. Martha is serving the meal, and Lazarus, whom Jesus recently raised from the tomb, is reclining with Jesus at the table.

   • **How would you picture the atmosphere at this banquet?**

Invite group members to picture a festive atmosphere in which Jesus and his friends are celebrating Lazarus's return from death. We can only imagine what a joyous time it must have been.

> *b.   What does Mary do?*

Mary anoints Jesus' feet with expensive perfume and then wipes his feet with her hair (see also John 11:2). Pure nard was a very costly perfume derived from a plant from India; it was worth about a year's wages (12:5).

Note: Some group members may know that the other gospel accounts also include a story of a woman annointing Jesus with expensive perfume. The accounts in Matthew 26:6-13 and Mark 14:3-9 are almost identical to each other, and these two accounts share quite a few details in parallel with the account in John 12:3-8. A reading of all three, however, also reveals quite a few differences. Another account in Luke 7:36-50 has similarities as well as other differences.

As we noted in Part One of this study, if group members raise questions about the difference of details in gospel accounts, it may help to note that this doesn't mean the Bible contains "mistakes." While it may even be possible to harmonize details from different accounts so that they logically fit together into one story, we need to be aware that seamless harmony and accuracy of detail weren't as important to the original writers as we might prefer today. The gospel writers were mainly concerned with sharing the good news of Jesus, and each writer had a particular audience in mind. Inspired by God, they related the stories of Jesus in ways that communicated the good news message effectively to their intended audience. Today we can still share in the good news of these accounts as we accept their central message by faith.

> *c.   Describe Judas's behavior in response to that of Mary.*

Judas objects to Mary's act of devotion, saying it's a waste of money that could be given to the poor.

- **What motivates each of them?**

- **How do we know Judas is not sincere?**

Mary is apparently motivated by wholehearted gratitude to Jesus. Nothing she could do would repay Jesus for raising her brother, Lazarus, from the grave. Her gift of expensive perfume is simply a sign of her appreciation and devotion. Her act also shows humility because in that culture it was usually the work of a servant or slave to care for someone's feet.

Judas seems at first to be motivated by a desire not to waste resources and to help provide for people who are poor. But John explains, "He did not say this because he cared about the poor but because he was a thief" (12:6). A thief cares not so much for others as for him- or herself. So Judas's motivation is mainly selfishness. John adds that Judas, as keeper of the disciples' money bag, often helped himself to the group's funds. In addition, we know Judas is not wholly devoted to Jesus because he will later betray Jesus. As we learn in Matthew 26:14-16, Judas soon offers to hand Jesus over to the Jewish authorities for money.

Note: Be aware that much speculation has developed about Judas's character and motivations. Some books and movies have portrayed him as a helpless pawn of the devil or as a misled political zealot who expected Jesus to free the Jews from Roman oppression. The Bible supports neither of those speculations. If group members want to discuss the matter further, you might invite them to look at other passages about Judas on their own (Matt. 26:14-25, 47-50; 27:1-5; Mark 14:10-11, 43-46; Luke 22:3-6, 47-48; Acts 1:15-19) and then discuss those together at another time. You might also indicate that you'll have the opportunity to discuss Judas again in lesson 4. Avoid speculation by noting that the Bible simply doesn't give us all the details about Judas, especially with regard to his destiny.

2. *John 12:7-11*

   a. *How does Jesus interpret Mary's actions?*

   • **Is Mary aware of Jesus' upcoming burial?**

Jesus states that Mary has saved the perfume for his burial and is now anointing him beforehand to prepare for that (see Mark 14:8). Whether Mary truly understands this as part of her act of devotion is debatable, but Jesus apparently saw her action as prefiguring his anointing for burial. In this way he defends Mary from the insincere and insensitive comments of Judas Iscariot.

   b. *Given the way Jesus has treated people in need, what does he mean in his remarks about the poor?*

   • **Why would he say, "You will always have the poor among you"?**

Jesus is not being insensitive to poor and needy people; he is merely quoting Deuteronomy 15:11 to state a fact: "There will always be poor people in the land." In other words, as long as there is sin and unrighteousness (injustice) in this world, there will be people who are poor and oppressed because of the selfishness of others.

Jesus constantly showed his care for the poor by providing many of them with healing, encouraging them with the good news of the kingdom of heaven, and rebuking the rich for ignoring them (Luke 4:18-19; 6:17-21; 7:22; 11:41-43; 14:13). He also often warned the rich that it was hard for them to enter the kingdom of heaven (Luke 6:24-26; 16:19-31; 18:24-25). In addition, Jesus himself had few possessions and lived the life of a relatively poor person.

In the context of his anointing at a dinner given in his honor, Jesus seems to be saying that expenses that are intended for celebrating and honoring God have a place even in this broken world—and perhaps especially because such celebrations help point us to the enjoyment of the full life God promises in his kingdom forever. Recall that we observed this point earlier when we discussed Jesus' first miracle, in which he changed water to excellent wine for a wedding banquet (John 2:1-11).

In addition, Jesus could have mentioned that Judas's criticism was merely selective. After all, couldn't the expense for the dinner have been used instead for the poor as well? But neither Judas nor anyone else seemed unhappy about attending this dinner "given in Jesus' honor" (12:2).

Godly living calls for caring for poor and needy people in various ways, and Jesus teaches that when we care for people in need, he sees it as caring for himself (Matt. 25:37-40). But this doesn't mean we can't celebrate or commemorate God's goodness at times along the way.

- **What can we do in our daily lives to maintain a healthy (godly) balance between caring for others and celebrating God's goodness? Between using our resources to help others and spending for ourselves?**

c. *What do the chief priests plan to do? Why?*

The chief priests and other religious leaders are concerned that Jesus is growing too popular. They reason that if raising Lazarus from the dead has given Jesus more credibility as the Messiah and has increased the number of his followers, they will have to kill Lazarus as well as Jesus.

- **What does their desire to kill Lazarus tell us about them?**

It shows not only their desperation and ill will—not to mention their hypocrisy as leaders of God's people—but also their blind determination to destroy Jesus. (See John 3:19-21; 9:39-41.)

- **Why are they bothered by the response of the crowd?**

The religious leaders will not tolerate anyone who might take away their power over the people and their position of favor with the Roman authorities (11:48).

3. John 12:12-16

a. *How does the crowd in Jerusalem greet Jesus and why?*

Jesus is received by a large, enthusiastic crowd. Many people have been traveling to Jerusalem to celebrate the feast of Passover, and word has spread quickly about the raising of Lazarus and other amazing signs Jesus has given to reveal himself as the Messiah.

- **Why do the people wave palm branches?**

Joseph Ryan describes the meaning of this tradition as follows: "During the two hundred years before Christ, waving leafy branches from the many palm-like trees in Israel had become a nationalistic symbol, like waving a flag. It demonstrated the people's hopes for a national liberator, a redeemer, someone who would rescue them from foreign oppression." The waving of palm branches had symbolized victory since the time of the Maccabean revolt in which the Jews defeated their Greek oppressors in 164 B.C. and were able to rededicate the temple in Jerusalem (see "Feast of Dedication" in glossary).

- **What does the crowd shout?**

The crowd quotes phrases from Psalm 118:25-26, part of a great praise psalm that calls for the waving of branches in a "festal procession up to the horns of the altar" in the temple (Ps. 118:27). "Hosanna" is a Hebrew expression that means "Save now" or "Give victory now" (see 118:25).

Psalm 118 was traditionally sung by Jewish pilgrims on their way to the Passover celebration in Jerusalem. The *Zondervan NIV Bible Commentary* notes that the crowd's words in John 12:13 ascribe "to [Jesus] a messianic title as the agent of the Lord, the coming king of Israel."

b. *What's the significance of the way Jesus rides into Jerusalem?*

John reports that Jesus "found a young donkey and sat upon it" for his entry into Jerusalem. (For additional details on this event, see parallel accounts in Matt. 21:1-11; Mark 11:1-11; Luke 19:29-44.) For a brief but more detailed account, you may wish to read Mark 11:1-11 with your group during this discussion time. In the Middle Eastern culture of that day, riding on a horse would have meant coming in a warlike manner, while riding on a donkey would have meant coming in peace (see Zech. 9:9-10).

Jesus, then, is riding into Jerusalem as a king. Though not everyone understands his mission, Jesus does not resist the celebrative spirit and enthusiasm of the crowd. After all, he is their Messiah, as he has been saying openly for almost six months since the Feast of Tabernacles (John 7). So he accepts the crowd's praise even though they generally misunderstand that he is not a political messiah.

Jesus knows, however, that the people's adulation is only temporary. In fact, in the book of Luke we read that he weeps for the city of Jerusalem and its people because they do not understand what will bring real peace, and he foresees that the city will be destroyed by invaders (Luke 19:41-44). He knows that many of the people will not ultimately believe in him and will face suffering in the future without the peace he can give. (Just over thirty years later, in A.D. 70, Rome's armies built an embankment and destroyed Jerusalem as Jesus predicted.)

   c. *When did Jesus' disciples understand the meaning of all this? Why?*

*   **What does it mean that "Jesus was glorified"?**

*   **How did the disciples learn what "had been written about him" in the Hebrew Scriptures?**

John points out that Jesus' disciples didn't understand the meaning of his riding on a donkey or even his mission as Messiah until "after Jesus was glorified." The *NIV Study Bible* explains as follows in a later text note (on 12:41) about glory: "The thought of glory here is complex. There is the idea of majesty, and there is also the idea . . . that Jesus' death on the cross and his subsequent resurrection and exaltation show his real glory." In other words, even Jesus' closest followers didn't fully understand his mission until after it was complete. After Jesus' crucifixion and resurrection they were still looking for him to be a political messiah (see Acts 1:6), even though he'd "explained to them what was said in all the Scriptures concerning himself" (Luke 24:27). Not until Jesus had ascended to rule in heaven and the Holy Spirit had come at Pentecost did they really understand what Jesus had been teaching and showing them (Acts 1:7-9; 2:1-39; Phil. 2:9-11). Note that we'll talk more about the Holy Spirit when we look at Jesus' promises in John 14 and 16.

4. *John 12:17-19*

   a. *How did the raising of Lazarus influence the crowd?*

*   **What did people do when they heard about Lazarus rising from the dead?**

In some ways the people were on the right track as they paraded with Jesus as their Messiah. They were looking for signs of the Messiah's coming, and they could see that Jesus was revealing those signs as he healed the sick, gave sight to the blind, and raised the dead (see Matt. 11:5). So the people spread the word about Jesus, and many came out of the city to meet him as he was approaching from Bethany. The raising of Lazarus was just one of many messianic signs, but it convinced many people that Jesus must really be the promised Messiah. The only problem, as we've often noted, was that the people were looking for a political messiah to rout their Roman oppressors. But Jesus had come to free people of all nations from the tyranny of sin and death, offering full life with God for all who would believe in him as Savior.

   b.   *Why were the religious leaders so frustrated?*

   •   **How were recent events affecting them?**

   As we have noted before, the religious leaders could sense their power and influence slipping away from them. Jesus' increasing popularity threatened their position as rulers of the Jewish people. They refused to believe in him as Messiah because he didn't fit their idea of what the Messiah should be (see John 5:16-18; 6:41-42, 52, 66; 7:27, 52; 8:23-27, 47-59; 10:22-33). And yet they likely realized that if he really was the Messiah, they would have to submit to him. So the only way they could see out of their predicament was to try to destroy Jesus.
   The leaders' frustration at this point echoed their sentiments from when they'd first heard that Lazarus had been raised from the dead: "What are we accomplishing? . . . Here is this man [Jesus] performing many miraculous signs. If we let him go on like this, everyone will believe in him, and then the Romans will come and take away both our place and our nation" (11:47-48). Now that Jesus was parading into Jerusalem to the praises of great crowds that had gathered for the Passover feast, the religious leaders were getting desperate. They were convinced they had to act quickly.

Questions for Reflection
In what ways can you show your devotion to Christ?

If you had been in the crowd when Jesus rode into Jerusalem, how do you think you would have responded?

Lesson 3
John 12:20-50

Drawn to True Life

Additional Related Scriptures

Psalm 89:36; 110:1-4
Isaiah 6:3, 8-13; 9:6-7; 49:5-7;
   52:13-53:12
Daniel 7:13-14

Mathew 10:39
Luke 23:20-23
John 5:19-30; 6:35-40; 8:12-47; 9:4-5;
   10:25-30; 11:9-10

Introductory Notes

In the Scripture passage for this lesson, Jesus talks about people believing in him and being drawn to him. We meet Greek believers who want to know more about Jesus, and we learn that "many even among the [Jewish] leaders" believe in Jesus but are afraid to stand up for him (12:42). These are people whom the Father is gradually drawing to himself (John 6:44), and Jesus explains that this process calls for him to be "lifted up from the earth" (12:32), meaning he will die on a cross for the sake of all who will believe in him as Savior (see 3:14-16).

Give thanks together that although we are weak-willed and often fearful, Jesus came to stand up for us. He came to take our place by suffering and dying for our sin. Because of Jesus' faithfulness, we are able to change radically to serve God instead of ourselves, and we are able to enjoy the gift of eternal life—to the Father's glory.

Optional Share Question

Tell about a time when you met someone important. Who was it, and what effect did that meeting have on you?

1. *John 12:20-26*

   a. Who wished to see Jesus, and why didn't they approach him directly?

     • **Why were they worshiping at the Passover Feast?**

     • **Why would they approach Philip?**

     • **What did they say to Philip?**

Several Greeks (Gentiles) wished to meet Jesus. These people were most likely God-fearing non-Jews who had rejected the pagan gods of Greece and

Rome and were attracted to the God of Israel. Groups of these "God-fearers" would sometimes come to Jerusalem and worship during religious festivals (see also Luke 7:1-9; Acts 8:26-39; 10:1-8). These individuals and others like them were allowed to worship in the area of the temple called the Court of the Gentiles—the place Jesus had cleared of merchants and money changers earlier (John 2:12-17).

We're not told exactly why these Greeks wanted to see Jesus. In the wake of Jesus' entry into Jerusalem on a donkey (12:12-19), these visitors likely wanted to ask him some important questions about God and faith. Perhaps they'd also heard of Jesus' amazing miracles and teaching throughout Galilee, a region where many Gentiles lived, and wanted to ask if he really was the promised Messiah. They may well have wondered how the Messiah's coming would affect them as Gentiles.

Philip, one of Jesus' disciples from Galilee, had a Greek first name. Perhaps especially because they were a minority group among the large crowds of Jews gathered at Jerusalem for the Passover, these Greek believers felt more comfortable approaching Jesus through Philip.

b. How did Jesus respond?

John doesn't indicate whether Jesus had a conversation with the Greek believers. Instead, we are simply told that when Philip and Andrew told Jesus about the Greeks' request, he responded by predicting that his death was coming soon.

- **What was the meaning of Jesus' illustration about a kernel of wheat?**

- **What was Jesus referring to as he spoke about the kernel, or seed, that dies?**

Jesus often used illustrations that applied to the agricultural society of his day. The people knew that seeds had to be dried in order to be planted so that a new plant could grow and produce more seeds. In this illustration Jesus was explaining that it would take the death and resurrection of one person (himself), to bring life that would produce many more believers in God. So Jesus was reminding his followers to think about the life to come, not just the here and now.

c. What does it mean to "hate" our life and "keep" it for eternal life?

Jesus was using an exaggeration technique (hyperbole) to get people's attention. He was saying that people who love this life and the world's system of self-centeredness will lose their opportunity to have true life, eternal life, because their focus is only on their own interests in this temporary life. People who "hate" this life, however, reject temporary values and follow Jesus' call to serve him with joy and purpose for eternal life.

- **What does it mean to serve and follow Christ?**

As Jesus pointed out, a person must commit to the values of God's kingdom as taught and lived out faithfully by Jesus.

- **What is the benefit of following Christ?**

The benefit is life forever in God's presence with Christ. In this way God the Father honors all who follow the Son, Jesus. In God's strength we can die to the ways of this world and begin bearing fruit that lasts forever (John 15:5, 8; Gal. 5:22-23). In fact, our eternal life begins when we become believers in Christ (John 5:24; 10:28-29; 2 Cor. 5:17).

- **What benefits do we enjoy already as believers in Christ?**

2. *John 12:27-33*
    a. *Why was Jesus troubled, and what was his prayer?*

Because he became fully human, made like us in every way except that he was sinless (Heb. 2:17; 4:15), Jesus naturally dreaded his coming death, knowing he would suffer in agony and terror. Still, he knew he had to go through with that to fulfill the purpose of his coming. He had to give up his own life to pay the penalty for human sin. His death and resurrection would glorify God, so he prayed, "Father, glorify your name!" (John 12:28).

    b. *How did God respond?*

The Father spoke from heaven, saying, "I have glorified it, and I will glorify it again" (12:28). By this the Father meant that Jesus' perfect life, including his faithful teaching and amazing miracles, had given glory to God, and that Jesus' death and resurrection would give God further glory.

- **What did the voice sound like?**

- **What confirmation and benefit came by way of the voice from heaven?**

The voice from heaven, which sounded to some people like thunder and to others like the speech of an angel, confirmed the Father's love and support for Jesus. Jesus noted that the voice was for the people's benefit, implying that this was an opportunity for them to believe.

Note: This is one of three places in the gospel accounts in which God speaks with "a voice . . . from heaven" (12:28). The first time was at the baptism of Jesus when he began his teaching ministry (Matt. 3:17; John 1:33). The second was at Jesus' transfiguration, which helped prepare and strengthen him for his journey to the cross (Luke 9:35, 51).

    c.   What did Jesus tell the crowd?

- **Who is the prince of this world, and how would he be driven out?**

Along with saying that the voice spoke for the people's benefit, Jesus declared that "the time for judgment on this world" had come; "the prince of this world"—that is, the devil—would "be driven out" by Jesus' sacrifice for sinners and his victory over death (John 12:31). Jesus would accomplish this by drawing people to himself when he was "lifted up from the earth" (12:32), as he had told Nicodemus earlier (3:14-15). John then explains that Jesus "said this to show the kind of death he was going to die" (12:33).

- **What kind of death would Jesus die?**

Jesus would die by crucifixion, the Romans' preferred method of execution for criminals. People were crucified by being lifted up on a heavy pole that had a crosspiece on which their arms were tied or nailed down. Their feet were also nailed or tied down against the pole. This terrible form of execution eventually gave rise to a word we still use to describe mind-numbing, body-wrenching pain: *excruciating.*

3.   *John 12:34-36*
    How did the crowd respond to Jesus' announcement?

The people were dismayed that while Jesus claimed to be the Messiah, he said he would soon be leaving. Naturally, they began to wonder about this, since the Scriptures taught that "the Christ will remain forever" (12:34; see Ps. 89:36; 110:1-4; Isa. 9:6-7; Dan. 7:13-14). *Why, then, was Jesus talking about being lifted up from the earth?* the people wondered. What's more, Jesus' talk about being the Son of Man mystified them. They were growing uncertain of his identity.

- **What did Jesus say next?**

Jesus responded with words similar to those he used earlier to teach his disciples about making the most of the time they had with him (see John

9:4-5; 11:9-10). Referring to himself again as "the light," Jesus urged the people to put their trust in him so that they could become "sons of light" (12:36) or "children of light" (see Eph. 5:8-10). Soon the light would be taken from them, Jesus explained, and if they did not understand that he was "the light of the world" (John 8:12; 9:5), they would fall into darkness.

- **What does it mean that darkness could overtake them?**

When people have no light, they are surrounded by darkness, overtaken by it. Jesus was saying that if the people did not follow him while they could, the darkness of this world would surround them and overtake them, and they would easily fall prey to the despair and hopelessness that results from slavery to sin and death (see John 8:34).

- **How can we apply these words of Jesus to life in our world today?**

- **Why did Jesus hide himself from the crowd?**

Commentators usually cite two possible reasons: either Jesus hid himself from those who wanted to arrest him, or he wanted to hide from those who wished to make him king.

4. *John 12:37-43*

   a. *What reason does John give to explain why many of the people in Jesus' day refused to believe in him?*

- **How did the prophecies from Isaiah apply to Jesus' situation?**

- **Does this mean people really have no choice to believe?**

This question opens a can of worms that could lead to theological debates about God's sovereignty and people's ability to believe. So you'll want to steer clear of arguing obscure points while trying to focus on the Scripture here.

As we've noted in earlier discussions, most of the Jewish leaders and the people who followed them refused to believe in Jesus as the Messiah, even though he did many amazing miracles, taught in amazing ways, and often clearly claimed to be the Son of God (see John 5:16-18; 6:41-42, 52, 66; 7:27, 52; 8:23-27, 47-59; 10:22-33; 11:46-48; 12:19). In addition, the large crowds of visitors in Jerusalem who had applauded him when he rode into Jerusalem were beginning to reject him and would soon call for his crucifixion (Luke 23:20-23).

John cites Isaiah 53:1 and 6:10 to explain the unbelief of most of the Jewish nation in response to Jesus. John even states, "For this reason they could not believe," indicating that God gave the people over to their doubts and unbelief. In other words, God had closed the door of faith to them—at least for a time—because they chose to remain in unbelief.

It's essential to note that people's unbelief is not God's choice. People start out in unbelief because they are born with a sinful nature and are literally slaves to sin (John 8:34). Then, at some point in their life, God opens the door to faith and free life so that they have an opportunity to believe (6:40, 44). While the door is open and the light is with them (8:12; 9:4-5; 11:9-10; 12:35-36), the people have a choice. But if they continually choose not to believe, God will eventually close that door and leave unbelievers in their unbelief.

God opens the door because he loves us and wants us to be saved. But if God closes the door, it's because we have refused God's love and decided to go our own way forever.

Be sure also to mention that God does not close the door to faith quickly. God loves us so much that he gives us a life full of opportunities to believe and be saved. Even though John mentions in this passage that God closes the door of faith on the unbelieving crowds in Jerusalem, we see later that the people also have other opportunities to believe—especially after Jesus rises from the dead, goes to heaven, and pours out the Holy Spirit on his followers. Even while Jesus is dying on the cross, as we learn from Luke 23:42-43, one of the criminals who is crucified with him believes and is saved.

Commentator F. F. Bruce adds that the "Hebraic [Jewish] fashion of expressing a result as though it were purpose has influenced John's wording. . . . Not one of [the people in Jerusalem that day] was fated to be incapable of belief; it is made plain below [see John 12:42] that some in fact, did believe. But the [Old Testament] prediction had to be fulfilled, and fulfilled it was in those who, as a matter of fact, did not believe." (See also Isa. 6:8-13.)

- **Can you look back and identify opportunities you were given to believe in Jesus? Can you tell how often you rejected him before believing in him? Explain.**

- **Think of people you know who do not know Jesus. In what ways does this discussion open our eyes to see that they need to see and believe in God's love?**

- **What can we do to keep showing people God's love and pointing them to Jesus?**

- How could Isaiah see Jesus' glory, especially since he lived about 700 years before Jesus came?

Isaiah the prophet saw Jesus' glory in visions and revelations from God. Isaiah's prophecies about the suffering servant of the Lord, for example, give descriptions not only of Jesus' suffering but also of his glory (see Isa. 49:5-7; 52:13-53:12). Note that in Isaiah 6:3 the prophet also describes a vision of the glory of the Lord Almighty.

b. *Why did the leaders who believed in Jesus fear the Pharisees?*

- What would happen to them if they declared their faith in Jesus?

Although the leaders who believed in Jesus were "many," they were apparently intimidated by the outspoken legal experts (Pharisees) and prominent priests (Caiaphas and others—11:49-50) who were part of the Jewish ruling council. As we discussed in our study of John 9, where we saw that the parents of a healed blind man were also afraid to speak up for Jesus, the ruling council had the authority to put people "out of the synagogue" (John 12:42), cutting them off from community privileges that included teaching, worship, marriage, and burial (see 9:22, 34).

- What does it mean that these believers "loved praise from men more than praise from God"?

The threat of disgrace and isolation from the community they had enjoyed all their lives would have been overwhelming for these Jewish believers. On their own, they didn't have the strength to stand up against the legalists and traditional lawkeepers of the Jewish community. Here we can see that, in a sense, even the traditional community of God's people enslaved those whom God was drawing to himself. But God would keep drawing them, as we will see. Even before Jesus rose from the grave, two of those leaders stepped forward to take Jesus' body down from the cross and place it in a tomb for burial (John 19:38-42).

Note together that faith in Jesus is something that requires strong commitment. Even more important, it requires God's strength. It takes God's strength to reject the false values of a society and take a firm stand for faith in Christ. The world laughs at Jesus, claiming he is no more than a fool or a lunatic (see 1 Cor. 1:18-2:16). But God's wisdom reveals the strength of his love, and God's Spirit provides the strength needed to express true faith in that love.

- In what ways can you identify with the believers' fears?

- Think of believers in Christ who face danger in countries that are predominantly Muslim or communist. In what ways can we support those believers in Jesus' name?

5. *John 12:44-50*

   Note: In the closing verses of John 12 we find a summary of teachings that Jesus gave earlier (see John 5:19-30; 6:35-40; 8:12-47; 10:25-30). If you're running short of time as you wrap up this lesson, you may want to summarize the main points here and ask group members to limit discussion to questions they might have on certain details.

   a. *What happens when a person believes in Jesus?*

   - **What does Jesus mean when he says that seeing him is the same as seeing the one who sent him?**

   Jesus says that whoever believes in him also believes in the Father, who sent him. The testimony of the Father and Son are the same. In fact, Jesus expands on this by saying that whoever sees him also sees the Father. He picks up on this topic again later in a discussion with Philip (see John 14:8-9). In other words, Jesus is saying that he and the Father are one (as in 10:30). In connection with this, Jesus adds again that he came to bring God's light into this world so that all who believe in him can find the way out of darkness.

   b. *What does Jesus say about judgment?*

   Jesus says he does not judge unbelievers and that he has not come into the world to judge it but to save it. This is similar to his statement in John 3:17: "God did not send his Son into the world to condemn the world, but to save the world through him."

   - **But if Jesus does not judge, why does he say that his word will condemn people?**

   Group members may recall other statements in which Jesus says he has the authority to judge and that he does pass judgment (5:26-30; 8:15-16), so they might wonder if there is a contradiction here. Note that Jesus makes all of these statements in connection with saying that he acts on behalf of the Father and that he and the Father are one. Though God the Father is usually identified in Scripture as the Judge of all people, we can see that Jesus' identification with God would also mean Jesus is Judge, as some other passages indicate (2 Tim. 4:1, 8; James 4:12; 5:7-9). In addition, note that not only Jesus but also God the Father is often identified as our Savior

(Ps. 25:4-5; 89:26; 1 Tim. 1:1; Titus 1:3-4; Jude 25). This doesn't mean, of course, that God the Father died on the cross; only God the Son did that.

While Jesus' meaning in John 12:47-48 may not be readily clear to us, scholars note that in this context he is emphasizing his role as Messiah/Savior and focusing on the purpose of his coming to save sinners. Judgment or condemnation is an *effect* of his coming, but it is not the *purpose* of his coming. In fact, judgment would occur even if Jesus hadn't come, for all people were lost in sin before he came (Rom. 3:10-12, 23).

The *NIV Study Bible* includes an illustration that you may find helpful in discussing this matter: "[It's] not the purpose of Jesus' coming, but judgment is the other side of salvation. It is not the purpose of the sun's shining to cast shadows, but when the sun shines, shadows are inevitable."

    c.   Who directs Jesus' teaching?

Jesus' teaching comes directly and entirely from the Father.

- **Why is this significant?**

Jesus wants to make clear that his teaching is entirely from heaven. He says this to assure the people that their Messiah is always doing the will of God.

Question for Reflection

Now that you've studied the second half of John 12, reflect again on the people's reactions to Jesus and what it might have been like to have been there. How do you think you would have responded to Jesus?

Lesson 4
John 13

An Example of Love

Additional Related Scriptures

Leviticus 19:18
Deuteronomy 18:21-22
Psalm 41:9; 51:2, 7
Isaiah 1:16-20
Matthew 26:14-35
Mark 12:30-31; 14:12-31
Luke 9:44-45; 18:31-34; 22:7-34, 69-70

John 7:33-36; 11:33; 12:6, 16, 23,
    27-28, 41; 14:16, 26; 16:7-14; 15:16,
    26-27; 17:1, 6-19, 20-23; 19:26; 20:2
Acts 1:6-9; 2:31-36
Romans 5:8, 10
Philippians 2:6-15
1 Peter 5:8
Revelation 12:7-12

Introductory Notes

We all have had jobs that we think are beneath us. But Jesus considered no job too low for serving as an example of God's love. In John 13 we find the amazing episode in which Jesus took a basin of water and a towel and washed his disciples' feet. These moments were among his last hours with his disciples, and he wanted to provide an indelible picture of true servanthood.

In this passage Jesus also predicts his painful betrayal by Judas as well as Peter's denial of him. Jesus felt the pang of rejection even within his circle of closest followers, all of whom eventually left him to complete the hardest part of his mission alone. Whenever we go through the pain of rejection or betrayal, we can be assured that Jesus knows our pain—and that he cares.

As John 13:1 explains by way of introduction, this section covers Jesus' final evening with his friends (John 13-17) as well as his death and resurrection:

> It was just before the Passover Feast. Jesus knew that the time had come for him to leave this world and go to the Father. Having loved his own who were in the world, he now showed them the full extent of his love.

Optional Share Question

What kinds of jobs do you avoid? Why?

1. *John 13:1-3*

   Describe the setting portrayed in these opening verses of John 13.

   • **When did this episode occur?**

   • **What facts are in the forefront of Jesus' mind?**

   As we've noted in the Introductory Notes above, John 13:1 describes the setting as "just before the Passover Feast," the event during which Jesus knows he will die as "the Lamb of God, who takes away the sin of the world" (John 1:29). In 13:2, John describes what immediately follows as taking place at "the evening meal." John's later descriptions of this meal and Jesus' predictions of betrayal and denial (John 13:18-38) show that this is most likely the Passover meal described in the other gospel accounts and referred to as the Last Supper and the Lord's Supper (see Matt. 26:17-35; Mark 14:12-31; Luke 22:7-34).

   John also notes that the devil had already tempted Judas to betray Jesus (13:2) and that Jesus knew his mission would soon be complete. Then he could return to the Father, who had sent him (13:1, 3). On this night and in the events of the next few days Jesus was ready to show "the full extent of his love" (John 13:1). You might also point out that some other Bible versions translate this phrase more literally as "he loved them to the end."

   • **How would you describe this love?**

   The love that Jesus displayed was sacrificial love that showed amazing compassion, care, mercy, and obedience to the will of God. This love led him all the way to death on a cross and beyond that to victory over death for our sake (see Phil. 2:6-15).

   • **Who were "his own who were in the world"?**

   Here John is probably referring to Jesus' closest disciples who still believed in him, but we can also see that this phrase could apply to all who would have faith in Jesus as Lord and Savior (see John 17:20-23).

2. *John 13:4-17*

   a. *What did Jesus do here for his disciples, and why?*

   Jesus assumed the place of a servant and began to wash his disciples' feet. He wanted them to understand the meaning of serving one another (see 13:12-16).

   In those days people's feet would get dirty from walking in sandals on dusty roads. Whenever people arrived at a home, it was customary for a servant to wash their feet—in much the same way that we offer a visiting traveler the opportunity to wash, rest, or freshen up. It's important to know, as well, that a Jewish servant would never be expected to wash the feet of another Jew. Only a Gentile slave would be required to do such a task. This made Jesus' willingness to wash his disciples' feet all the more shocking.

So Jesus was showing his disciples how much he loved them, and he was modeling true humility by using this act as a symbol of how far he would go to show his love. This act of service demonstrated his willingness to give of himself sacrificially for them, despite their sinfulness (see Rom. 5:8, 10).

Note: In Luke 22:24 we read that the disciples were arguing about which of them was the greatest. Notice the connection between that episode and the footwashing scene recorded in John. In both episodes Jesus discusses how his followers are to be like servants rather than masters or rulers who lord it over others.

> b. *Why did Peter resist at first?*

Peter was probably embarrassed that Jesus, their Lord and Teacher (13:13), would humble himself in this way. Peter likely thought that Jesus should not lower himself to a servant's role.

- **Can you identify with Peter?**

- **How do you think you'd respond if Jesus came to you today and washed your feet or shined your shoes or cleaned up a mess you made?**

Use some questions like these to help group members understand Peter's surprise and responses in this scene. Though he believed in Jesus as the Messiah, Peter didn't yet understand what Jesus would do for all believers (13:7). Peter likely pictured the Messiah as a great earthly ruler, just as many other Jews did (see Acts 1:6). So Jesus' act of footwashing was completely out of character even for a great, benevolent earthly king. But, as we know today, Jesus was far more than that. He is King of the universe, he is Lord, and his glory shines brighter than the sun and all stars put together. So it can be extremely surprising and humbling to think of this King doing something menial for us today—and yet that's what he does, watching over us and loving us in our weakest and even our proudest moments.

> c. *What changed Peter's mind? Why did he need to allow Jesus to wash his feet?*

Jesus made Peter think again when he said Peter would have no part with him if Jesus didn't wash him. While Jesus' action was symbolic of his love and servanthood for his followers, his washing of their feet also symbolized his ability to wash away their sins (see Ps. 51:2, 7; Isa. 1:16-20).

- **Why did Peter say Jesus should wash his hands and head as well?**

This episode gives us some insight into Peter's generally impetuous, rash character. He sometimes swings from being totally noncompliant to being overly accommodating. Perhaps he is so overwhelmed by Jesus' gesture and Jesus' response that he wants to show he'll do whatever it takes to remain Jesus' disciple. What he doesn't realize is that only Jesus can do this for him. F. F. Bruce puts it this way: "In his impetuous reply, Peter shows that he has not grasped the deeper import of his Master's action; the external washing symbolizes something inward, and the washing of the feet alone can symbolize it just as well as the additional washing of the hands and face would do."

d. Who was clean and who was not? Why?

Note together that Jesus washed the feet of all his disciples, including Judas, who would soon betray him.

- **What made Judas unclean? Was it his sin in plotting to betray Jesus, or was it his unbelief?**

Group members may give various answers, but in this context it appears that Jesus was referring to unbelief as uncleanness. The distinction between Judas and the others at this point was his unbelief and his willingness to be rid of Jesus. All of the disciples, of course, needed to be washed clean of their sins, but Judas's sin of betrayal apparently stemmed from his unbelief.

e. What else did Jesus say to explain his washing of everyone's feet?

Jesus wanted his followers to know they should serve each other without trying to promote themselves at the expense of one another. They needed to learn the lifestyle of servanthood and humility.

- **What does it mean to "wash one another's feet" (13:14)?**

In the kingdom of God this means simply to serve each other and to show God's love to everyone, as God does. *Note:* While some churches regard footwashing as a sacrament in which they actually wash one another's feet, most do not follow the practice literally. Jesus' main point here is to provide an example of servanthood (13:15).

- **What did Jesus promise for those who followed his example?**

Jesus promised his followers that if they humbled themselves and served others as he did, they would be blessed.

- **Can you think of a time when you figuratively washed someone's feet?**

Encourage group members to share some of their experiences in helping other people.

- **In what ways were you blessed?**

3. *John 13:18-30*

  a. What's the significance of the Scripture that Jesus quoted here?

Point out that in John 13:18, Jesus quotes from Psalm 41:9. This psalm is a deeply emotional expression of Israel's King David, composed at a time when he was betrayed by a close and trusted friend. The words reflect the frustration and anguish this type of betrayal can cause. Jesus quoted this psalm of David to show that Scripture was being fulfilled—and it reflected what he was going through. Judas had been a trusted friend and close companion throughout the years of Jesus' teaching ministry. He had witnessed all the amazing things Jesus had done, and he'd been trusted with the group's money bag (John 12:6).

  b. What explanation did Jesus give about what would soon happen?

Jesus explained that he was predicting his betrayal so that when it happened, the disciples would know he was truly the Messiah, the Son of God. We could interpret this explanation in at least a couple of ways: (1) Because Jesus told them what would happen in the future, his disciples would know he was a prophet when the prediction came true (see Deut. 18:21-22). (2) When they later saw and understood all that Jesus had to go through to save them, including being betrayed into the hands of his enemies, Jesus' disciples would know he was truly the Son of God, the Savior of the world, as he had said (see Luke 9:44-45; 18:31-34).

Note again Jesus' use of the emphatic "I am" in John 13:19, pointing to his claim to be God. We'll discuss this expression and its meaning in more detail when we study John 14 in lesson 5.

c.   *How did Jesus as well as his disciples react when he said this?*

- **What does it mean that Jesus was troubled?**

D. A. Carson points out that the Greek word for "troubled" signifies revulsion, horror, anxiety, and agitation. Clearly it was no small thing for Jesus to look into the future and see the pain and suffering that lay ahead for him. (See also John 11:33; 12:27.)

- **What did the disciples do?**

They stared at each other, surprised and completely uncertain about which of them Jesus was referring to as his betrayer.

- **Who was the disciple whom Jesus loved?**

Throughout this gospel account this person remains anonymous, but by process of elimination and with other clues regarding Jesus' three closest disciples—Peter, James, and John—it becomes clear that this person is the gospel writer John (see 19:26; 20:2; 21:20-24).

- **How did Jesus reveal the identity of the one who would betray him?**

Jesus said he would dip a piece of bread and hand it to his betrayer. He then did so, giving the bread to Judas Iscariot.

- **What does it mean that Satan entered into Judas?**

John uses these words to indicate the extent of Judas's betrayal and to show that while Judas is fully responsible for his actions, the Lord's battle against sin and death cut to the heart of the spiritual forces of evil in this world. This was so serious a battle that "the prince of this world"—Satan—would soon "be driven out" (12:31), and, as we can imagine, the devil wasn't about to take this sitting down (see 1 Pet. 5:8; Rev. 12:7-12). Taking full advantage of Judas's openness to betray Jesus for money (Matt. 26:14-16), Satan made his move to influence this betrayal as much as he could. Try as he might, however, the devil couldn't change God's plans to save us from sin. It's true that Jesus would be betrayed and killed. But as Jesus himself pointed out (John 13:18), this was to fulfill the Scripture in which God's salvation through the promised Messiah was prophesied many years earlier.

As we have noted before, it's important to point out that Judas was not an innocent victim (see comments in lesson 2, under question 1c). Some in your group might ask whether Judas had any other choice but to betray

Jesus. While some interpreters have made this a matter for extensive discussion, the biblical record is brief and shows that Judas was responsible for his actions. So it's wise to avoid speculation about Judas as well as about his ultimate destiny, which we can entrust to God.

- **Why were the disciples so clueless about Judas's motives?**

Look back together at the disciples' surprise in John 13:22 after Jesus says to them all, "I tell you the truth; one of you is going to betray me" (13:21). Jesus had mentioned this to them before, as noted in other gospel accounts, and on each occasion they did not understand what he was talking about (Luke 9:44-45; 18:31-34). Recall again that the disciples didn't really understand Jesus' entire mission till after it was complete, so it was natural to assume that Judas, who had charge of the money, had simply gone out to buy something rather than to betray Jesus into the hands of his enemies. Even "the disciple whom Jesus loved" apparently didn't understand the impact of Judas's leaving at that moment (John 13:28), though Jesus had shown this disciple that Judas was the betrayer (13:26). This disciple simply didn't have the insight at the time to see that Jesus' betrayal and death were so close at hand.

Note also, if necessary, that John wrote this account some years after the events took place (probably not before A.D. 50), so by that time he'd been able, with the Holy Spirit's help, to sort out the impact of these events, all of which happened rather quickly in these final hours of Jesus' teaching ministry.

Considering that John often mentions light and darkness in line with Jesus' teaching about being the light of the world, you may wish to add the following observation: regarding the statement "And it was night" (John 13:30) the *New Bible Commentary* adds, "It may well be that John intends more than a comment on the time. It was spiritually night for the soul of Judas."

4. *John 13:31-38*

   a. *What did Jesus mean when he spoke about God and the Son of Man being glorified?*

- **What connection did this have with Judas's departure?**

Again Jesus was talking about his upcoming crucifixion and resurrection, which would glorify God the Father as well as the Son (Jesus) by making our salvation possible. Recall together earlier discussions about Jesus' being glorified (see John 12:16, 28, 41; see also Phil. 2:6-11).

Judas's leaving to betray Jesus meant that it would now be only a short time till he would be arrested and then crucified. As the drama unfolded,

45

Jesus was showing he was aware of each development along the way (recall his announcement in John 13:21) and that the appointed time for his sacrifice as the Lamb of God was near (see 12:23, 27; 13:1; 17:1; see also 7:6, 30; 8:20).

- **What does verse 33 tell us about Jesus' feelings for his disciples?**

As their Teacher and Lord (13:14), Jesus served as a father figure for his disciples, and here he calls them his children. Note together that Jesus had chosen these disciples for special training during his teaching ministry. He had described himself earlier as their shepherd (10:11-15, 27-30), and he would soon pray for them as the ones God had given him to protect and nurture in faith (17:6-19).

Note: The Greek word for children here is *tekna*, which literally means "little children." This is the only time the word occurs in John's gospel account, but John uses it seven times in the letter we know as 1 John.

- **Where was Jesus going?**

He was going to the cross to die and to return to his Father in heaven. After rising from the dead, he would also later ascend to heaven and rule at the Father's right hand (Luke 22:69-70; Acts 1:9; 2:31-36). See also Jesus' comments in John 7:33-36.

- **Why couldn't the disciples follow him?**

As the *New Bible Commentary* puts it, "glorification would involve separation." The disciples and other believers would join Jesus in heaven someday (John 13:36), but for the time being they needed to stay behind and tell the world about him (13:35; 15:16, 26-27).

b.   What command did Jesus give his disciples, and how was it new?

In a sense, the call to love one another was not new. In Leviticus 19:18 God had taught the people of Israel, "Love your neighbor as yourself" (see Mark 12:30-31). But Jesus added a new condition when he said, *"As I have loved you, so you must love one another."*

- **What is the difference between loving your neighbor "as yourself" and loving as Jesus has loved you?**

The love of Jesus was new to the human experience because Jesus displayed the ultimate sacrificial love. Jesus, who became human for us, came to serve us and give his life for our sake—even when we were his enemies (Rom. 5:8, 10). This is completely unconditional love.

- **How could the disciples express Jesus' kind of love?**

The disciples could follow Jesus' example in all they said and did by demonstrating servanthood, sacrifice, empathy, care, concern, and much more. As the disciples would learn later, they couldn't do any of these things without the strength of God the Holy Spirit working in them, but Jesus promised that the Spirit would come after he returned to the Father (John 14:16, 26; 16:7-14; Acts 1:8).

c. *How did Peter view his loyalty to Jesus, and what did Jesus say about it?*

- **What did Peter want to know?**

Peter wondered why Jesus said no one could follow him. Believing he would follow Jesus wherever he would go, Peter claimed he was willing to lay down his life for Jesus.

- **What prediction did Jesus give?**

In response to Peter's rash claim, Jesus questioned his disciple's loyalty and predicted that, instead, Peter would disown Jesus.

- **When would this happen?**

Jesus said Peter would disown him three times before the rooster crowed—that is, before sunrise the next morning.

- Have you ever made rash promises that turned out quite differently? If so, how did that make you feel?

Question for Reflection
What can we learn from the words and actions of Jesus in the episode covered in this lesson? From the words and actions of the disciples?

Lesson 5

John 14

"I Am the Way and the Truth and the Life"

Additional Related Scriptures

Exodus 3:14-15; 12:1-42; 20:7;
33:17-23
Leviticus 24:16
Matthew 10:3
Mark 3:18
Luke 6:16

John 1:29, 32-34; 3:16; 4:21-24;
5:17-40; 6:35-58; 7:37-38; 8:12, 34;
9:5; 10:7-18, 24-30, 37-38;
11:25-26; 12:26, 44-50; 13:12-19,
21, 28, 34; 15:1, 5, 12-17; 16:7-15
Acts 1:13; 2:1-4:22
Galatians 5:13-16, 22-25
Philippians 2:6-11

Introductory Notes

In this lesson we find words of tremendous comfort in the midst of
important teachings. Jesus spoke these words first to his disciples, but these
sayings have provided comfort to all generations of Jesus' followers.

It was the night before he was crucified, and Jesus said to his followers,
"Let not your hearts be troubled. Trust in God; trust also in me" (John 14:1).
Then he proceeded to teach about his going to prepare a place for them in
heaven, saying, "I am the way and the truth and the life. No one comes to
the Father except through me" (14:6). Jesus had made several other "I am"
statements before, and we'll be exploring those in some detail in this lesson.
As we've mentioned in earlier lessons, Jesus' use of this construction made
clear to his listeners that he was claiming to be God. And in the statement he
makes here he sets himself apart from all other religious leaders. This is the
teaching from which the Christian church learns that belief in Jesus is the
only way to eternal life with God.

In the Scripture for this lesson Jesus also introduces the Holy Spirit as
"the Counselor" who will come to be with his followers after Jesus goes
away (14:16, 26). It's important to know that the word for "Counselor"
(*parakleton*) in this passage can be translated more literally as "Comforter."
With these words of comfort Jesus' disciples also receive a glimpse of the
close relationship between the persons of the Trinity—Father, Son, and Holy
Spirit—and how they work together to provide us the assurance of God's
love and peace and eternal life.

Optional Share Question

Describe what comes to mind when you think of heaven. Believers often talk about the assurance of meeting their deceased Christian friends and loved ones in heaven someday. But even though that will be wonderful, how do you think it will compare to meeting Jesus, the Word of God, the Son of God, who loves us so much that he came to die for us so that we could live with him there?

1. *John 14:1-4*

    a.   Why did Jesus tell his disciples not to be troubled?

Jesus knew the disciples would be disturbed by his discussion about leaving them. Recall together the events described in John 13, noting that Jesus' conversation with them here is a continuation of the one begun in that chapter.

- **What did he want them to do instead?**

Jesus wanted them to trust in him as well as in God the Father. All their lives his disciples had been taught to trust in God. So here Jesus was reminding them to do that, and he was making clear that they could count on him as well, because, as many scholars have noted, he was implying again that he is not only human but also God (as we'll see more clearly in his next "I am" claim in verse 6). Jesus had come to show God's love to his people. In fact, he had become human in order to do that—not only to be like us but also to die in our place. Knowing what lay ahead of him in the next twenty-four hours, Jesus was teaching his followers that his mission would prove him worthy of their trust—and yet he knew they needed comfort because they couldn't grasp these events in the way he could.

    b.   What does Jesus promise to provide for his disciples?

Jesus tells his disciples he is going to heaven, his "Father's house," to prepare a place for them. The *NIV Study Bible* points out that the "many rooms" Jesus refers to are literally "'dwelling places,' implying permanence." Jesus also indicates that he will come back and take his followers to heaven.

- **What does he mean when he says he will come back for them?**

The exact timing of Jesus' return is not specified, but the timing is not as significant as the event itself. The *New Bible Commentary* notes that this comment is most likely a reference to the second coming, when Jesus will return at the end of time (see John 6:40, 44), "but some have interpreted it as referring to [Jesus'] resurrection or to Pentecost or even to a coming at the death of believers." This last interpretation refers to a belief that when a believer dies, Jesus comes back to escort the person's soul to heaven—but this belief has no biblical basis. It may be a spin-off of a Jewish rabbinical teaching that Jesus himself referred to in a parable about a poor man who died and was carried off "to Abraham's side" by angels (Luke 16:22).

- **How would the disciples know the way to the place Jesus is going?**

The disciples have been following Jesus and listening to his teachings, so they should know that the way is simply to follow him (John 6:35-58). In addition, Jesus has just told them that he will go and prepare a place for them, so the natural route would be through Jesus and by following his teachings. But here, as in other situations, the disciples don't understand.

2. *John 14:5-11*

   a. *What does Thomas claim, and how does Jesus respond?*

Thomas appears to be either confused or stubborn. He claims that the disciples do not know where Jesus is going, so he asks, "How can we know the way?" (14:5).

Jesus explains with the powerful statement "I am the way and the truth and the life. No one comes to the Father except through me" (14:6). He also points out that if the disciples really know him, they will know the Father as well. Then Jesus announces that "from now on," they do know the Father, because they have seen Jesus, who represents the Father in every way (5:17-30; 6:38; 10:25-30; 12:49-50).

- **What does Jesus mean when he says, "From now on you do know him and have seen him"?**

Jesus is saying that once the disciples realize who he is and that he is in the Father and the Father is in him (see 10:38; 14:11), they will finally understand his teaching. In other words, anyone looking at him will see and know the Father, because Jesus has done everything according to the will and word of the Father (5:17-30; 12:49-50).

   b. *Why would Jesus make such an exclusive claim (v. 6)?*

- **If Jesus and the Father are one (John 10:30), why wouldn't Jesus be the way to the Father? Who else has this kind of relationship to God Almighty?**

If we examine the Scripture leading up to this point, we can see that Jesus is leading up to this claim throughout his teaching ministry. Though he hasn't stated it as directly as he does here, he has stated it in various ways, all of which lead to the same conclusion (see 5:22-30; 6:39, 44-51; 7:37-38; 8:12; 10:7-18, 27-30; 11:25-26; 12:26, 44-46; 13:19).

- **Why does Jesus have the right to make such a claim?**

Jesus has the right to make this claim for several reasons. As we have discussed in earlier lessons, Jesus is who he says he is—the Messiah, the Son of God who came from heaven to save God's people from their sins (Matt. 1:21). In addition, the Father and the Scriptures and John the Baptist have testified about him (John 1:32-34; 5:33-40). So have Jesus' miracles and teaching (5:36; 10:25, 37-38). Jesus has even testified about himself (10:24-25). But Jesus doesn't "lord it over" anyone to believe in him (see Luke 22:25). He earns the right to make this claim by setting an example: coming to serve, living a perfect life, and laying down his life so that all who believe in him may have eternal life (see 3:16; 6:40; 10:11-18; 13:12-17, 34; 15:12-17). Although the disciples were still confused about the example Jesus was giving them, they would understand after his mission was complete and the Spirit came to "teach [them] all things" (14:26).

As we have noted in earlier lessons, Jesus' use of the phrase "I am" was a clear reference to his identity with God (John 8:12; 9:5; 10:7, 9, 11, 14; 11:25; 13:19; 14:6; 15:1, 5). Long ago God had revealed himself to Moses, naming himself as "I AM WHO I AM." By this name God identified himself as "the LORD . . . the God of Abraham, the God of Isaac and the God of Jacob," saying, "This is my name forever, the name by which I am to be remembered from generation to generation" (Ex. 3:14-15). This covenant name of God came to be revered as so holy that the Israelites wouldn't even say it or write it out, apparently fearing they might misuse the Lord's name (see Ex. 20:7; Lev. 24:16). Instead they referred to it in their Scriptures as *yhwh*, commonly known today as *Yahweh* (also *Jehovah*) and designated in most English Bibles as "the LORD" (with large and small capital letters).

When God sent Moses to demand freedom for his people Israel, Pharaoh the king of Egypt refused to believe in Moses' God or to bow to him. But eventually God showed that he was Lord of all the earth and had power even over death, so Pharaoh finally relented and freed God's people from slavery. That was the night of the Passover (Ex. 12), which the people were celebrating again many years later as Jesus spoke these words to his disciples. Note together the amazing connections between God's name, the Passover and deliverance from slavery (see also John 8:34), and Jesus' claim as he prepares on this final Passover evening to become "the Lamb of God, who takes away the sin of the world" (1:29).

c. *What is the meaning of Philip's request in verse 8?*

• **Does this seem unreasonable or disrespectful, considering that he's been with Jesus for so long?**

Philip wants more proof than Jesus' word. He wants a clear demonstration of God's presence. At first glance, Philip's question might seem to be born of stubbornness or even arrogance (as Thomas's question may seem). But as we see Jesus answer his disciples patiently, we can tell that they simply don't understand most of what he is teaching them. We have to remember that they have not yet witnessed Jesus' death, resurrection, and ascension and that they won't understand all this till the Holy Spirit comes to "guide [them] into all truth" (John 16:13). In fact, they are probably still reeling from Jesus' announcement just a few minutes earlier that one of them will betray him (see 13:21, 28).

In addition, the request for a clear revelation of God was something that a number of Old Testament people had made as well. For example, Moses asked to see God's glory, and yet God gave him only a glimpse so as not to harm him (Ex. 33:17-23).

• **How does Jesus respond?**

Jesus challenges Philip by saying, "Don't you know me . . . ?" (John 14:9). At this point Philip simply does not see the Father in Jesus. The Lord goes on to say that his words and works are the words and works of the Father. Then he adds that if Philip cannot believe Jesus' words at this point, he should "believe on the evidence of the miracles" he has seen and realize that these miracles have come from God.

3. *John 14:12-14*
   a. *What does Jesus tell his disciples they will be able to do?*

• **What reason does he give for this?**

Jesus says that anyone who believes in him will be able to do what he has been doing—and even greater things than that. This will happen, he says, because he is "going to the Father." We learn later that God's plan involves the coming of the Holy Spirit after Jesus' ascension. The Spirit will empower Jesus' followers with knowledge, understanding, and even gifts of healing—all for the glory of God (John 16:7-15; Acts 2:1-4:22).

- **What could the "greater things" be?**

Commentator F. F. Bruce offers the following insight: "This promise indeed came true: In the months after his death and resurrection many more men and women became followers through [the disciples'] witness than had done so during [Jesus'] personal ministry in Galilee and Judea." This widespread belief in Jesus came as a result of the Holy Spirit being poured out over the whole church (body of believers) after Jesus had finished his mission as Messiah.

    b. What great promise does Jesus give in verse 13?

Jesus promises that he will do whatever his followers ask in his name, so that he may bring glory to the Father.

- **What condition is attached to this promise?**

The condition is that Jesus' followers ask *in his name,* implying an intimate connection with him that honors the will of God. F. F. Bruce comments, "If something is asked for in Jesus' name, the request is probably viewed as addressed to the Father. The Father denies nothing to the Son, and a request made in the Son's name is treated as if the Son made it."

- **Does this mean we can get anything we want by using Jesus' name?**

People often misunderstand this statement of Jesus. It doesn't mean that only prayers asked "in Jesus' name" will be answered, nor that we can get what we want simply by including these words in our prayers. Using Jesus' name for selfish purposes would be a *misuse* of the name of God (see Ex. 20:7). As faithful followers of Jesus, we are called to be sincere and to seek God's will in our prayers. Commentator Leon Morris explains this way: "This does not mean simply using the name as a formula. It means that prayer has to be in accordance with all that the name stands for. It is prayer proceeding from faith in Christ, prayer that gives expression to a unity with all that Christ stands for, prayer which seeks to set forward Christ himself."

4. *John 14:15-27*

    a. What will result if the disciples love Jesus?

    b. How will this connect with the work of the Holy Spirit?

If the disciples love Jesus—that is, if they believe in him as Lord and Savior—the result will be obedience and intimacy with God. The test of love is wholehearted obedience, and if people are truly followers of Jesus, they will do what Jesus commands.

- **How will Jesus' followers be able to obey?**

They will be able to do this through the gift of "the Counselor, the Holy Spirit" (John 14:26), who comes to be with them, live in them, and teach them all things.

- **What does Jesus mean when he says he will not leave his disciples "as orphans"?**

Even though Jesus is leaving his disciples, he will not leave them helpless. He will send the Counselor to guide, protect, and teach them. The Counselor, the Holy Spirit, will never leave them.

- **When will the disciples realize that Jesus is in the Father? Why?**

The disciples will see the truth of Jesus' identity after his death and resurrection. When the Holy Spirit comes to live in them and teach them, they will see that Jesus has been in the Father and the Father has been in him.

- **Why does Jesus says the disciples will be in him and he will be in them?**

Jesus wants the disciples to know they will have an intimate relationship with him and with the Father. In many ways their relationship with God will be like Jesus' relationship with God. With the Spirit's guidance, they will be obedient to God, in tune with God's will, and enjoy the peace of God's presence with them (14:27).

- **What does Jesus mean when he says that he will show himself to his disciples?**

He means, again, that the Holy Spirit will reveal the truth and identity of Jesus to them.

c. *How does "Judas (not Iscariot)" respond, and what does Jesus say to him?*

- **Who is this other disciple named Judas?**

Very little is known about this disciple. His name is mentioned in Luke 6:16 and Acts 1:13, which indicate that he was the son of someone named James. He is probably also the same person who is called Thaddeus in Matthew 10:3 and Mark 3:18.

This disciple, like the others, doesn't understand fully what Jesus is saying, so he asks why Jesus would show himself only to them and not to the world.

Jesus assures Judas and the others by saying that God will come to anyone who loves Jesus. Through the Holy Spirit, both Jesus and the Father will come and make their home with that person.

- **Why is this important?**

Jesus' answer here indicates that his message is for the entire world and not simply for one group or nation. Recall again Jesus' comments in John 3:16; 4:21-24; and 10:16.

- **Why does Jesus again say the Father is the source of his words?**

In verse 24 Jesus again points to the Father to show that his teaching has the authority of God. Jesus is indicating that his disciples need to listen and take care to obey his words, for they are the words of God.

d. *What kind of peace is Jesus promising in verse 27?*

The peace Jesus offers is unique in that it is not like the peace the world offers. Jesus' peace is not merely freedom from conflict; it is also anxiety-free and phobia-free. This is true peace that frees us to live in step with the Spirit of God (see Gal. 5:13-16, 22-25). It gives a genuine, meaningful, and everlasting sense of well-being. This is the peace known as *shalom* to the people of God.

- **How does Jesus again indicate his compassion here?**

Jesus concludes this section of his teaching with the same words he used earlier: "Do not let your hearts be troubled. . . ." In this way he shows his ongoing compassion for his followers. Reflect together on the vast number of believers who have experienced Jesus' compassion and peace in all sorts of circumstances throughout the ages.

- How can Jesus' words to his disciples here be a source of comfort and peace to us today?

5. *John 14:28-31*

   a. *Why would the disciples be glad that Jesus is going away?*

When he has gone away, the disciples will know more about Jesus' identity as well as his full purpose in coming. They will see that he is "the way and the truth and the life" (14:6). The Holy Spirit will help them understand Jesus' relationship with the Father and the importance of his teaching, which comes from the Father. The Spirit will also reveal that Jesus has been glorified by providing salvation for us and being raised from the dead to rule at God's right hand in heaven (see Phil. 2:6-11).

- Won't Jesus' followers be in danger from "the prince of this world"?

- What impact will the "prince of this world" have on Jesus?

- In what way will this information comfort the disciples?

When Jesus says, "The prince of this world is coming," he means that Satan will display his power especially in Jesus' betrayal, arrest, trial, persecution, and crucifixion. But Jesus adds that the devil will have no hold on him. In other words, Satan's power will be limited to do only what the Father allows in order to accomplish salvation for sinners who believe in Jesus. Jesus is assuring his disciples that they will have nothing to fear in the face of the devil's power, for Jesus' and the Father's power is far greater.

   b. *What must the world learn about Jesus? Why?*

The world must learn that Jesus, the Son of God, loves the Father and has done exactly as the Father has commanded, which will include giving up his life and allowing himself to be persecuted by the devil for our sake. In this way Jesus will provide the only way for people to be saved.

Questions for Reflection

How can we share with others the essential truth that Jesus is the only way to salvation?

What can we do to share the peace of Christ with others?

Lesson 6
John 15

The True Vine

Additional Related Scriptures

Psalm 35:19; 69:4; 109:3
Isaiah 5:1-7
Jeremiah 12:2, 10
Ezekiel 19:10-14
Matthew 21:33-41
John 1:1, 14; 3:19-20; 6:44; 11:48;
    12:32, 37-40; 13:16, 34-35; 14:6,
    12-16, 21-26

Acts 1:8; 7:54-8:3; 9:1-2
Romans 12
1 Corinthians 3:11-15; 12:1-31
Ephesians 2:10; 4:7-16
Galatians 5:22-25
1 John 4:19

Introductory Notes

Jesus knew that his time with his disciples was short. Within a few hours he would be arrested and sentenced to be crucified, so he wanted to give his followers some important words of instruction, warning, and comfort. Many of these words repeat teachings he gave earlier, but in this passage Jesus offers great comfort by describing himself as "the true vine" (John 15:1) to which all believers can remain connected through the life and guidance of the Holy Spirit. Jesus knew the challenges his followers would face when he was arrested and crucified, and he knew how they would struggle and persevere in God's strength in the years ahead.

Optional Share Question

Think of a time when you received correction from a teacher, coach, or other mentor that turned out for your good. What did you learn?

1. John 15:1-8

    a. Explain the word picture Jesus uses in these verses.

- **Who does the vine represent?**

- **Who is the gardener?**

Vines and vineyards are often used as metaphors in the Bible to describe God's relationship with his people (see Isa. 5:1-7; Jer. 12:2, 10; Ezek. 19:10-14; Matt. 21:33-41). In this passage Jesus shapes the metaphor to describe himself as "the true vine" and God the Father as the gardener who tends the vine. Fruit growers know that their vines and trees need constant pruning in order to produce well.

- **Why does Jesus call himself the "true vine"?**

Jesus is the true vine because real life, eternal life, is possible only through him. All branches and fruit depend completely on the vine for nourishment, strength, and support.

- **Who are the branches?**

The branches are people, who depend on Jesus and the Father for life and productivity.

- **What does Jesus mean when he says the disciples are already clean?**

This means the Father has already pruned them so they will bear good fruit. The disciples have already listened to Jesus' word—his teaching—so a pruning process is under way in their lives. Note that an NIV footnote explains, "The Greek for *prunes* also means *cleans.*"

- **What does this tell us about "the word"?**

If a person listens to the word or message of Jesus, it brings changes and challenges that can prune, shape, and clean up that person's life for bearing fruit for God. Recall together that Jesus himself is also "the Word" (John 1:1, 14).

- **What is the fruit Jesus is talking about?**

The fruit represents productivity for good in one's life—good works done out of gratitude for all God has done in Christ. In fact, the vine is the source of all good works that the branches produce. We'll talk more about fruit when we discuss verse 16 of this passage.

b.   What does it mean to remain in Jesus?

When Jesus says, "Remain in me," he means, "Stay with me; maintain an ongoing connection with me." He's describing our closeness to him in very personal terms, and he promises to stay connected with us—an amazing offer, considering who Jesus is!

- **Why do we need to stay connected with Jesus?**

Jesus points out that fruit will automatically develop and grow when a person stays connected with him. But if there is no connectedness, no fruitfulness will result.

- **What does Jesus mean when he says, "Apart from me you can do nothing"?**

If Jesus is not a vital part of our lives, we cannot do anything that will ultimately last. Again, we'll talk more about "fruit that will last" when we discuss verse 16.

- **What are some ways we can stay connected with Jesus?**

We learn more about God and desire to stay connected as we read and study God's Word, communicate with God through prayer, and reflect on what God has revealed in creation. We also find that the Holy Spirit continually encourages us to maintain this connection—and this is evidence of Jesus' remaining connected with us.

Note: A question may come up about branches that are cut off and thrown into the fire. If people have difficulty with this concept, it may help to point out that Jesus is talking about branches that have, in a sense, already cut themselves off from the vine. They have not remained in the vine, so they are disconnected and thus do not bear fruit. They are like the people Jesus describes in John 3:19-20 who refuse to come into the light because they love the darkness. They love doing things their way and don't want God to come into their lives and change them. If necessary, remind everyone also that this is only an illustration to help us see our vital connection to Jesus; it doesn't speak to all our questions about the way God saves people.

c. *What is the condition for the promise in verse 7, and what is the result?*

Repeating a promise made earlier, Jesus says we can ask for whatever we wish, and "it will be given" (15:7; see 14:13-14). The condition for this is essentially the same as in his previous discussion. Jesus says here that we must remain in him and that his words must remain in us, and earlier he indicated that our requests had to be in line with honoring his name, having faith in him, and showing our love for him by obeying his commands (14:12-15). The result—glory—is also noted in both discussions.

- **Who is glorified and why?**

The Father is glorified when we remain in Jesus and bear fruit. This shows that we are his disciples and that we understand the meaning and purpose of the Father's sending the Son into the world.

2. *John 15:9-17*

   a.   How has Jesus loved us?

- **What does this mean?**

Here Jesus expands on his teaching from John 13:34-35 and 14:15, 21-24. What an astounding statement! Jesus loves us in the same way the Father loves him. Recalling that Jesus is the Son of God who came from heaven to become one of us, we know this means we are loved wholeheartedly, unconditionally, and eternally. It means Jesus' love for us is comprehensive and complete.

- **How should this affect our view of ourselves?**

   b.   Why should we love each other?

Jesus calls us to love one another with unconditional love because this is the kind of love he has shown by his example, especially in his willingness to die for us. As John puts it in 1 John 4:19, "We love because he first loved us."

- **What is complete joy?**

Complete joy is the sense of peace and well-being we have in knowing we are loved by God. Joy is not mere happiness, which can be here today and gone tomorrow. It is rock-solid, based on the firm foundation of God's faithful love shown in Jesus.

- **What is a clear example of love for others?**

Jesus says there is no greater love than that of a person who gives up his life for his friends (15:13). As he speaks with his disciples here, Jesus is likely predicting what he will do for his friends—and for us all—within the next twenty-four hours.

- **How can we be friends of Jesus?**

- **What's the difference between servants and friends?**

We can be Jesus' friends and remain in his love when we do as he commands—namely, by showing love to one another through God's amazing power in us. Friendship does not put us on an equal footing with Jesus; it simply means we have a personal relationship with him. He invites us into this relationship and shows us the purpose of his mission, which is far more than a master would reveal to a servant (15:14).

c.   What has Jesus chosen us to do?

Jesus has chosen and appointed us "to go and bear fruit—fruit that will last" (15:16).

What is fruit that lasts?

This is fruit produced in and through us by the Spirit of God. These are good works that result from our gratitude to God for all he has done to save us and give us new life forever. The fruit of the Spirit, produced through the Spirit within us as we "keep in step with the Spirit" (Gal. 5:22-25)—or "remain in the vine" (John 15:4)—is fruit that will last.

- **Note Jesus' closing repetition of the command to love each other (v. 17). Reflect on and share some examples of this kind of love from your own experience.**

3.   *John 15:18-25*
   a.   What should we remember when the world rejects us?

Jesus points out that the world has rejected him, so we should expect the same treatment when we bring his message to the world.

- **Why does the world reject believers?**

The world rejects believers because Jesus chose them out of the world and they belong to him. Though most people who belong to the world are not aware of it, the world is a spiritual battleground in which the devil is furiously trying to destroy God's plans to save all who believe in Jesus and belong to him (John 8:23-24, 42-47; 12:31; 13:27; 14:30-31; see 1 Pet. 5:8; Rev. 12:7-12, 17). Recall an earlier discussion on this matter in connection with John 13:27. Note also that Jesus often reminded the religious leaders that they didn't know "the One" who sent him (15:21; see 5:37-38; 7:28-29; 8:18-19, 55); they hated Jesus because they were blind to the truth and refused to believe he was the promised Messiah (12:37-40; see 2 Cor. 4:4).

- **What does Jesus mean when he says, "No servant is greater than his master" (v. 20)?**

Whatever the master has to face, the servant must also face. So if the master has to face persecution, so will those who work for the master. Believers in Jesus should expect to be persecuted. (See also John 13:16.)

- **Why does the world persecute believers?**

Persecution is an extreme form of rejection, and it occurs because the world not only rejects believers but also despises them and wants to harm them. Persecutors are also often afraid of losing their position of power and status and the privileges it entails (see John 11:48).

b. Why is the persecution of Jesus and his disciples inexcusable?

The persecution by the Jewish establishment is inexcusable because Jesus came into the world to bring the people the truth about the Father and himself—and the Jewish leaders rejected him. This made them "guilty of sin" (15:22). Leon Morris explains, "Jesus does not mean, of course, that the Jews would have been sinless had he not appeared. But it does mean that the sin of rejecting God as he really is would not have been imputed to them had they not had the revelation of God that was made through him. But now, as things are, they have no excuse. There is no way of covering up their sin." (As you discuss this question with your group, you may want to refer back to comments about John 12:37-40 in lesson 3.)

c. What does Jesus mean when he says, "He who hates me hates my Father as well" (v. 23)?

Some group members may find it hard to accept that people hate Jesus and his Father. Even many people who follow other religions see Jesus as a good person. Some other religions claim to believe in God but not in Jesus as God. But Jesus is pointing out that anyone who rejects him rejects "the One" who sent him (15:21).

Jesus uses a strong word here—"hate"—to describe the result of not putting God the Father and Jesus first in our lives. When we remove the Father and Jesus (and the Holy Spirit) from their rightful place as Lord over all, we pretend to put ourselves or some other god (or ideology) in their place. This amounts to a complete rejection (or hatred) of the one true God.

- **How does this statement relate to Jesus' claim to be "the way and the truth and the life" (John 14:6)?**

Invite everyone to picture what often happens when people face Jesus' claim to be the only way to eternal life. Hatred of Jesus is not an uncommon reaction, especially when people realize that God allows no room for other beliefs or the worship of other gods (Ex. 20:1-6). Despite many claims to the contrary today, the worship of any god who is not the Father of Jesus is the worship of a false god.

- What kinds of reactions have you received when you've explained to people that Jesus is the only way to eternal life with God the Father, who sent him?

  d. *How does the world's hatred of Jesus fulfill the law?*

It may help to explain that the word "Law" in John 15:25 refers not only to the Ten Commandments but to all the Hebrew Scriptures, most of which make up the Old Testament in our Bibles today. You may also wish to read Psalm 35:19 and 69:4, noted in an NIV footnote as Scriptures that Jesus is referring to. Leon Morris points out that these two passages and possibly Psalm 109:3 speak of hatred that is irrational. As we have observed, the religious leaders hated Jesus although he showed clearly through his teaching and miracles that he was their Messiah.

4. *John 15:26-27*

  a. *What do we learn about the Counselor in this passage?*

As Jesus has mentioned before (see lesson 5), the Counselor will come to lead and guide God's people in truth and obedience, helping them understand all that Jesus has taught.

In this passage we also learn that the Spirit will be sent by Jesus as well as by the Father (see 14:16, 26).

  b. *Why must the disciples testify?*

The disciples must testify about Jesus because they have seen and experienced the truth from him personally. Jesus consistently told the truth throughout his teaching ministry, and in this statement he is giving them the responsibility of laying the foundation (foundational teachings) of his church.

- **What should Jesus' followers say?**

All believers are called to testify that Jesus is the way, the truth, and the life, sharing the good news of salvation everywhere (Acts 1:8). Note also that the testimony of Jesus' followers is the prime example of "fruit that will last" (John 15:16). In all we think, say, and do, we should be mindful of sharing the message and love of God, as Jesus did.

Questions for Reflection

What kinds of things need to be present in your life to help you remain in Christ?

With whom can you share the message and love of Christ today?

Lesson 7
John 16

The Counselor

Additional Related Scriptures

Matthew 16:15-19
Luke 24:27, 44-49
John 6:39-40, 69-70; 13:36; 14:6, 27;
  15:20, 26; 20:10-21:14
Acts 1:1-3; 2:1-4:37; 7:54-8:3; 8:26-40;
  9:1-2; 10:1-11:18; 13:1-3; 15:22-32

Romans 3:22-25
Colossians 2:13-15
2 Timothy 3:16-17
1 John 3:8
Revelation 19:11-22:5

Introductory Notes

Jesus continues to prepare his followers for the difficulties they will soon face when he is arrested and crucified. He compares their time of grief to a woman in childbirth, who labors in great difficulty for a time and then experiences great joy when her child is born. Jesus also again promises to send the Counselor, the Holy Spirit, who will come to be with them and live in them. The Spirit will supply them with peace so that the disciples may "take heart" when they face tough times; through the Spirit, Jesus' followers can be assured that he has "overcome the world" (John 16:33).

Optional Share Question

Describe a time when you received some advice or instructions that helped prepare you for a challenging situation later. What did you learn, and how did it help?

1. *John 16:1-4*
   What will soon happen to the disciples, and why does Jesus tell them this?

Jesus says that his followers will be kicked out of the synagogue and that they might even be killed, because extremists could easily believe they are doing God a favor by not simply persecuting them but also killing them. If you have time, you might review together what actually happened to the earliest followers of Christ (see, for example, Acts 7:54-8:3; 9:1-2).

- **Why will the religious leaders do such things?**

Again Jesus points out that his enemies do not know the Father and, as a result, they do not recognize Jesus (16:3). Also recall Jesus' earlier statement "'No servant is greater than his master.' If they persecuted me, they will persecute you also" (15:20).

- **Why does Jesus tell them all this?**

Jesus tells his disciples these things so that they will not go astray from serving God when they face these struggles. Note that the Greek word for "go astray" (*skandalizo*) is related to the word for "scandal" (*scandalon*). To wander from the faith for which Jesus will soon give his life would be scandalous, causing great offense to God.

Jesus adds that he is saying these things so that when they happen, his disciples will know they have been forewarned. He also indicates that as long as he is with them (16:4), they are under his protection. As we will see later, even as Jesus is being arrested he protects his disciples (John 18:4-9). But they need to be prepared for a time when people will think that persecuting Christians is necessary and is even "a service to God" (16:2; see Acts 7:54-8:3; 9:1-2).

2. *John 16:5-11*
   a. *Why will Jesus' leaving be good for his followers?*

While Jesus' departure might seem to leave his followers defenseless, it will ultimately be for their good. After Jesus' death and resurrection the Holy Spirit will come to live in them and help them understand all that Jesus has taught them. They will have redemption and the assurance that Jesus has taught the truth. They will also see that Jesus fulfills all the Old Testament prophecies about the Messiah (see Luke 24:27). In addition, the Spirit's coming will enable the disciples to go out on their own and spread Jesus' message of love and grace. The book of Acts shows that after the Spirit came, the disciples gained understanding and power to act in ways that were not evident when Christ was physically present (see Acts 2-5).

- **What does Jesus mean by saying, "None of you asks me, 'Where are you going?'" Didn't Peter ask this question earlier?**

Peter did ask this very question earlier, so it may seem strange that Jesus makes this comment. The *NIV Study Bible* offers this explanation: "Peter . . . asked such a question (13:36), but quickly turned his attention to another subject. His concern had been with what would happen to himself and the others and not for where Jesus was going."

b.   In what ways will the Counselor influence the world?

Jesus says the Spirit will convict the world of sin, righteousness, and judgment. All people who have yet to hear the good news and believe will be subject to this work of the Spirit. In other words, Jesus is talking about us and everyone else who has heard his message since the outpouring of the Spirit on Pentecost (Acts 2).

- **How does the Spirit do these things?**

The Spirit moves us to recognize that we are guilty of *sin* and in need of the Savior. We must confess our sins and ask for God's forgiveness, made possible through the finished work of Christ.

The Spirit also convinces us that we need to be *righteous* (blameless, without sin) before God. Because Jesus is the only human who is righteous and because he died in our place, God will consider us righteous for Jesus' sake if we have faith in him (Rom. 3:22-25; see John 14:6).

The Spirit convicts us of these truths by working in our hearts to help us learn God's Word to us in Scripture (2 Tim. 3:16-17). The Spirit also works through other believers to help us learn these things.

In addition, the Spirit makes it clear that if we are not credited with Jesus' righteousness through believing in him as Savior, we will face God's *judgment* for the consequences of our sins.

- **What does Jesus mean here when he mentions "going to the Father" and "the prince of this world" being condemned?**

Commentators note that Jesus' going to the Father signals God's approval of his righteousness and clarifies that "the prince of this world"— that is, Satan—is evil and has been judged (John 16:11; see Col. 2:13-15; 1 John 3:8).

3.   *John 16:12-16*
What will the Spirit of truth do for Jesus' followers?

Jesus tells his disciples the Spirit will guide them into all truth. When Jesus has left them, their source of truth will have departed, but the Spirit will come to live in them and help them understand all the truth Jesus has been teaching them.

- **How will the Holy Spirit accomplish this?**

The Spirit will speak only what he hears from the Father and the Son (see John 15:26). The Spirit will also tell them "what is yet to come" (16:13) in the future. You may want to refer your group to the book of Acts and point out some of the ways the Spirit led the early church (see, for example, Acts 2-4; 8:26-40; 10:1-11:18; 13:1-3; 15:22-32). You might also mention John's later visions about Jesus' coming again (Rev. 19:11-22:5).

- **How will the Spirit bring glory to Jesus?**

The Spirit will reveal the vital and essential points of Jesus' message to believers and to the world. The Spirit does this through Scripture and by guiding the church until Jesus comes again.

- **What does Jesus mean when he says, "All that belongs to the Father is mine"?**

Recall that Jesus is God the Son and that he said, "I and the Father are one" (John 10:30). Between the Father and the Son is a mutual sharing of love, grace, knowledge, lordship, and everything else that makes up their one being. Also note that the Holy Spirit shares in this unity.

- **What does verse 16 mean?**

Most likely Jesus is referring to his death and burial and then to his appearances after his resurrection (John 20:10-21:14). Some commentators suggest that the phrase "after a little while" may also refer to the coming of the Spirit or to Jesus' coming again at the end of time (see 6:39-40). Jesus also explains this further in the next part of his discussion.

4. *John 16:17-24*
   a. *What are the disciples wondering about here?*

- **Why do you think they're confused?**

Some of the disciples seem confused by Jesus' references to "going to the Father" and being seen again "in a little while." Indeed, as we've been discussing these things, we can see that Jesus' words can be hard to understand—and we have the advantage of the Spirit's teaching and nearly two thousand years of scholarship to help us. Note, as well, that the disciples may be completely overwhelmed by Jesus' teaching at this point. It probably has been no more than a few hours since he washed their feet and predicted his betrayal (John 13). In addition, the disciples likely still have strong notions about the Messiah being a political conqueror (see Acts 1:6).

b. How does Jesus respond to their confusion?

Jesus sees that they do not understand him, so he makes a comparison between their situation and that of a woman giving birth to a child. While the process is extremely painful, the joy of giving birth to a child helps the mother forget the anguish she has been experiencing. The loss of Jesus' presence will also be painful, but the gain that comes through his death and resurrection will give them such great joy that they will forget their anguish over losing him.

- **Why will the disciples weep and mourn while the world rejoices?**

When they become aware of his suffering and cruel death, the disciples will weep and mourn, but the unbelieving world will rejoice that Jesus is dead.

- **What does Jesus mean when he talks about *asking* in verses 23-24?**

The *NIV Study Bible* suggests that when Jesus says, "You will no longer ask me anything," he "seems to mean asking for information (rather than asking in prayer), which would not be necessary after the resurrection." Then he moves on "to the subject of prayer," teaching his disciples to make requests in his name—that is, in line with his message and God's will and in honor of all he has done, as we have discussed in earlier lessons. Commentator F. F. Bruce adds, "Access to the Father in Jesus' name was part of the joy which was promised."

5. *John 16:25-33*

   a. Why has Jesus been speaking figuratively to his disciples?

- **When will he speak plainly to them?**

Until the disciples' eyes are opened through the teaching of the Spirit, they won't grasp what he is saying. Even if Jesus spoke plainly to them all the time, they wouldn't understand his meaning. Even though he has explained some of his parables to them, the full meaning won't be clear until after his mission is complete. When he says, "A time is coming when I will no longer use this kind of language" (16:25), he is probably referring to the teaching he will do after his resurrection (see Luke 24:27, 44-49; Acts 1:1-3).

b.   What relationship do the disciples have with the Father?

Because the disciples have loved Jesus and believed in him, the Father loves them. We'll learn more about this privileged relationship with the Father when we look at John 17 in lesson 8.

- **What does Jesus say about his relationship with the Father?**

Jesus notes again that he came from the Father to enter this world and will soon return to heaven to be with the Father there.

c.   How do the disciples respond to Jesus' explanation?

They say that Jesus is speaking clearly and that they understand what he is saying. They appear to have fresh insight and vision into Jesus' identity and the fact that he came from God.

- **Reflect on what it might have been like to be in a discussion with Jesus. Would you have been intimidated, especially if you knew who he was? Do you think you'd have understood everything he was saying?**

d.   What does Jesus say next, and what does this mean?

- **Hasn't he already stated that they believe in him?**

Jesus and the disciples have spoken of their belief in him before (Matt. 16:15-19; John 6:69-70). But here he seems to be acknowledging that they have clearer understanding. F. F. Bruce comments that perhaps Jesus is reading their hearts and they are experiencing a moment of clear revelation.

- **How will the disciples respond to Jesus' arrest, trial, and execution?**

Jesus says they will scatter to their homes and leave him all by himself.

- **Will Jesus really be all alone at that time?**

Jesus notes that the Father will be with him during this time of severe distress and suffering.

e. What assurance does Jesus give in these parting words to his disciples?

Jesus says he has told the disciples these things so that they will have peace. This will be the peace he spoke of earlier (14:27); it's the *shalom* of God that will ultimately sustain them through the struggles they will face in the near and distant future. This peace will transform their fears into joy and thanksgiving. Jesus also adds, "Take heart! I have overcome the world" (16:33). When they face trouble in the future, the disciples will be able to recall and find strength in these words of assurance.

- **When we face situations that cause us to worry, how can these words comfort us? How can we take heart?**

- **What does it mean that Jesus has overcome the world?**

With this all-encompassing promise Jesus declares that he is in control and can give us true peace, whatever the world or the forces of evil may try to do against us.

Questions for Reflection

In what ways has Jesus prepared his followers for the challenges they will be facing?

How do his words prepare us as well?

Lesson 8

John 17

Final Prayers

Additional Related Scriptures

Psalm 20:1; 54:1
Proverbs 18:10
Matthew 6:9-13; 10:19-20
John 1:1-4, 10-14; 13:18-30; 15:8-16:4,
32-33

Acts 2:42-27; 4:32-35
Ephesians 2:6
Philippians 2:5-11

Introductory Notes

Perhaps you have known the comfort of being prayed for at one time or another. Perhaps a family member or friend has spoken to God on your behalf. You may even be aware that you've been prayed for countless times. In this lesson we have the privilege of listening to Jesus pray that God will work through him, through his disciples, and through all believers who will come after them. That includes all believers throughout the centuries—even us who are believers today. What's more, the Bible also teaches that Jesus and the Holy Spirit keep praying for us throughout our lives. Amazing! (See Rom. 8:26-27, 34; Heb. 7:25; 1 John 2:1.)

Optional Share Question

If you could bring one prayer request to Jesus, what would it be?

1. *John 17:1-5*

    a. *What does Jesus ask for in these verses?*

    Jesus asks God to glorify him so that he may give glory to the Father for giving him authority to grant eternal life to all believers.

    • **Is Jesus praying for himself?**

    Leon Morris writes in his commentary, "This is not a prayer for himself in the way we usually understand this. Since [Jesus'] glorification is to be seen in the cross, it is a prayer rather that the Father's will may be done in him. If we do talk about it as Jesus' prayer for himself, we should at least be clear that there is no self-seeking in it."

b. How does Jesus describe eternal life in this passage?

Though we often think of eternal life as life that lasts forever in the joy and wonder of God's presence, here Jesus describes it in terms of a relationship in which we truly know God.

- **With whom do we have this relationship?**

This relationship is with "the only true God" and Jesus Christ.

- **What does it mean to know this God?**

The knowledge Jesus is talking about seems to include the idea of deep and abiding love—not just head knowledge, but heart knowledge guided by faith that assures believers of God's truth to the core of their being. F. F. Bruce comments, "The Father and the Son know each other in a mutuality of love, and by the knowledge of God, men and women are admitted to the mystery of this divine love, being loved by God and loving him."

Invite your group to explore what it means to have a relationship with God.

- **What do the words "the only true God" imply?**

The only true God is the one revealed in the Old and New Testaments; this is the God who has sent Jesus to be the Savior of all sinners who believe in him as Lord.

As we've noted in past lessons, some group members may question this teaching or say that God as revealed through Jesus is the same in all religions but may have different names. Acknowledge that while many people today believe that all religions lead to the same God, it's important to investigate and compare what other religions actually say about God. For example, Buddha was not even certain there was a God; Jews, Muslims, and others say they believe in the God of Abraham but not in Jesus as the Messiah or as the Son of God who is fully human and fully God. The book *Jesus Among Other Gods* by Ravi Zacharias can be a helpful reference in this discussion.

c. What does Jesus acknowledge about himself in verses 4-5?

- **What do we learn about the relationship between Jesus and his Father?**

- **What is the work Jesus has completed?**

- **Is he talking in the past tense only? Why or why not?**

Jesus knows he is facing the cross and death, and he is speaking to his Father in very intimate terms. He discusses his work as if the entire mission is already completed. He also indicates that he had a preexisting glory with the Father. Though Jesus is about to suffer the humiliation of the cross, the end result will be the glory of conquest over death (see Phil. 2:5-11). You may wish to read John 1:1-4, 10-14 together again and reflect on it quietly before moving on to the next section of Jesus' prayer.

2. *John 17:6-12*

    a. What has Jesus revealed, and how has he done this?

Jesus has fully revealed the Father to his followers. Some translations say that Jesus has revealed God's name. What does this imply?

- **What does a name indicate about a person?**

Names in the biblical context often refer to a person's character, describing dominant personality traits or recalling an event that shaped the person's character. Leon Morris states that when Jesus revealed God's name, he revealed the "essential nature of God."

- **What have the disciples done with this revelation?**

Jesus says they have obeyed and believed the message he came to bring into the world.

- **Where do they believe Jesus came from?**

They have come to know "with certainty" that Jesus came from the Father and that therefore Jesus' message came from the Father as well. In other words, they trust the message Jesus has brought in the Father's name.

    b. Why is Jesus praying for his disciples but not for the world?

At this point in his prayer Jesus appears to be clarifying that he is praying for his disciples—probably because they are listening (see John 16:33-17:1). This doesn't mean he doesn't pray for or care about the world (see 17:21). Jesus is likely saying this simply to assure his disciples that he is praying for them as they are about to face the world's hatred and persecution for his sake (see John 15:8-16:4, 32-33; 17:13-15).

- Discuss the phrase "glory has come to me through them."

- What does this say about Jesus' view of his disciples?

- What does it mean to bring glory?

- Has this already happened, or is Jesus looking into the future?

Jesus saw the potential of the Spirit's work in his disciples. F. F. Bruce puts it this way, "He looked at them with the insight of faith, hope, and love and realized their present devotion and their potential for the future. In themselves they were weak indeed, but with the Father's enabling grace and the guidance and illumination of his Spirit, they would fulfill the mission with which they were now being entrusted and bring glory to their Master in fulfilling it." Bruce goes on to say that the verb tense indicates that Jesus is so confident of this that he expresses it as if it has already been accomplished.

On the matter of bringing God glory, you may want to review earlier discussions of this topic from lessons 1 and 3.

   c. *What does Jesus want for the disciples that he has experienced with his Father?*

Jesus wants protection for the disciples and asks that they may be one with the Father just as he and the Father are one. The unity of God—Father, Son, and Holy Spirit—provides the basis or model for the unity of God's people, the body of believers known as the church. We'll talk more about this oneness in our discussion of verses 20-23. Acts 2:42-47 and 4:32-35 show some examples of how this prayer was answered in the lives of the disciples and other early believers.

- How will the power of God's name protect the disciples?

- What power is there in a name?

God's name is holy, as Jesus makes clear in the address "Holy Father." And by virtue of God's powerful nature, God's name is powerful. As we can see later in verses 17-19 of this prayer, Jesus wants his followers to be sanctified, or made holy—that is, "set apart for service to God"—and this special calling includes a measure of protection. Jesus has had this protection during his teaching and healing ministry, and he is asking for it for his disciples. F. F. Bruce adds that the name of God in the Old Testament denotes God's power and protection as well as his character (see Ps. 20:1; 54:1; Prov. 18:10).

d. What does Jesus' prayer tell us about being kept safe and being lost?

Jesus says he has protected the disciples and kept them safe by the name God gave him. R. V. G. Tasker puts it this way: "While Jesus has been with them, the revelation of the holy Father given to them by the sinless Son has saved them from the corrosive and disintegrating power of evil."

Then Jesus speaks about one who was "doomed to destruction so that the Scripture would be fulfilled." This statement appears to be a reference to Judas, who has betrayed Jesus into the hands of his enemies. As we have noted earlier in this study, people have often speculated about the motives, actions, and destiny of Judas, but since the Bible doesn't support such speculations, we have to be content with its limited detail and trust that Judas's destiny is best left in Gods' hands. (You may wish to review your earlier discussion of this matter in lesson 4.)

Leon Morris offers these comments: "The disciples need not fear, for Christ had kept them, so that none was lost. And if attention be drawn to Judas, then the retort must be that the Father's will was done both in the eleven and in the one, for Scripture was fulfilled. He [Judas] was a responsible person and acted freely. But God used his evil act to bring about his purpose. There is a combination of the human and the divine, but in this passage it is the divine side rather than the human which receives stress. God's will in the end was done in the handing over of Christ to be crucified." (See also Acts 2:23.)

3. *John 17:13-19*
What do the disciples need to be protected from, and how will they be protected?

The world hated Christ, so it's natural that it would hate his followers. They therefore would need protection from the world. You may wish to refer your group to Matthew 10:19-20, which mentions some of these protections.

- **From whom specifically do they need to be protected? How?**

Jesus' disciples will need protection from the evil one (Satan), and God will protect them. By the power of the Holy Spirit living in them, they will become sanctified or "set apart" by the word of truth. In other words, Jesus is praying that they be equipped with the right message and the strength to serve God in holy obedience, giving glory to God (see vv. 6-10).

- **What is the full measure of the joy Jesus wants his disciples to know?**

He wants them to know the joy of doing the Father's will.

- What does Jesus pray regarding their relationship to the world?

- What implications does this have for how we relate to people around us?

Jesus does not want the disciples taken out of the world, because they will be the ones who take his message to the world. But while they remain in the world, he wants the Father to protect them from the evil one.

Some churches teach that we should separate ourselves from the world. But Jesus makes clear that his followers should remain where there are people who need to hear his message. Disengaging from the world may make it easier in some ways to be a believer, but disengaged believers will have little or no impact on the world and the message will not get out through them. Ultimately this disobedience leads to a wandering from God's mission and a weakening of the believer's relationship with God.

4. *John 17:20-23*

   a. Who does Jesus now include in his prayer, and what does he pray for them?

   - Describe the oneness Jesus is talking about here.

In verse 20 we can see that Jesus is praying for all believers—and that includes us. He wants all believers to be one, unified as one body in God's name, just as Jesus and the Father are one.

   b. What is the purpose of the oneness of all who believe?

Jesus wants believers to be united "to let the world know" that the Father sent him and has loved them just as the Father loves the Son. As you discuss this question, you may want to refer again together to John 3:16, 13:34-35, and 15:12 to review Jesus' teaching there in connection with this passage.

   - In what ways can believers live out this purpose on a daily basis?

   - What should make us different as we engage the world?

   - What will cause the world to believe?

Jesus knows that the actions of all who identify with him will have an influence on the world when people observe the unity of believers in his name. Ultimately a person comes to belief only by the work of the Spirit in his or her life, but we are called to be examples that help point people to Jesus and see God's amazing love and work in us. We are his witnesses

(Acts 1:8), so we must be mindful of serving in a unified way that mirrors the loving unity in the relationship between the Father and the Son.

- In what ways can Christians display this unity?

- What care should we take when discussing other denominations or Christian groups with people who do not believe in Jesus?

5. *John 17:24-26*

   a. What additional prayer requests does Jesus make on our behalf?

- What does it mean to be with him?

Jesus says he wants believers to be with him and to see his glory. Leon Morris comments that this is not a wish but a chosen course of action that Jesus knows will happen. He wills that we will be with him in all his splendor (see Eph. 2:6; Rev. 21-22).

- What is the glory Jesus mentions here?

   b. What will Jesus continue to reveal to those who believe in him?

Jesus promises to make God known to all believers.

- What does it mean to make God known?

F. F. Bruce notes that "by worldly standards of success Jesus had little to show for his mission. He had come to make the Father known, but the vast majority of his hearers refused the knowledge he offered them. The merest handful of men and women—a very unimpressive company at that—had recognized him as the sent one of God and had come to know the Father in him. Yet to them his mission on earth was confidently entrusted as he dedicated them to the Father to this end. They would know more about Jesus and his work and in that way God would be made known to them."

- What kind of responsibility does this place on us today as Jesus makes God known to us, and we in turn make him known to others?

The church, the body of believers in Jesus Christ, needs to be unified so that God's love can keep spreading throughout this world and being a righteous influence. Jesus wants the world to believe in him as the Savior sent by God to redeem the world (John 17:20) and bring people into God's family.

Questions for Reflection

What difference does it make in your life to know Jesus has prayed these prayers for you?

What can you do in response to Jesus' prayers and show the unifying love of God in this world?

As you close this lesson, you may want to invite everyone to turn to Matthew 6:9-13 and say the Lord's Prayer together. Invite everyone to look in the Lord's Prayer for parallels to the prayer in John 17, and urge everyone to give thanks each day for the Lamb of God who came to do God's will and bring salvation into this world.

Lesson 9
John 18

Jesus' Arrest

Additional Related Scriptures

Matthew 26:36-27:26
Mark 14:32-15:15
Luke 22:39-23:19

John 7:6, 30; 8:20; 10:39; 12:23, 27;
13:1; 17:1

Introductory Notes

John 18 begins with Jesus and his disciples going to an olive grove, where Judas soon leads the Jewish authorities to arrest Jesus. John leaves it to the other gospel writers to mention Jesus' anguish as he struggles there with God to let the suffering of the cross pass from him (Luke 22:39-46). During this time Jesus asks his Father if there might be another way to save the world, but this is one prayer of the Son to which the Father answers no.

The story of Jesus' passion shows that in his obedience he is willing to submit humbly to betrayal, torture, and even death. The religious leaders and Roman authorities may think they are in charge, but Jesus and the Father are truly in control. As Jesus said when teaching about laying down his life for his sheep, "The reason my Father loves me is that I lay down my life—only to take it up again. No one takes it from me, but I lay it down of my own accord. I have authority to lay it down and authority to take it up again" (John 10:17-18).

Although we will look primarily at John's account of Jesus' arrest in this lesson, you may wish to invite group members to look also at the other accounts in Matthew 26:36-27:26; Mark 14:32-15:15; and Luke 22:39-23:19.

Optional Share Question

Think of a time, perhaps in your childhood, when a friend betrayed you. Describe what you experienced.

1. *John 18:1-11*

   a. *How does Jesus show he is in charge of the situation surrounding his arrest?*

   John makes it clear that Jesus knows what's going to happen to him and that events will unfold according to his foreknowledge.

- **Why would Jesus go to a place where Judas and the authorities could easily find him?**

John notes that Jesus often met with his disciples in the olive grove where Judas brought the soldiers and officials to arrest him. If he didn't want to be arrested, he could have eluded the religious leaders, as he often did in the past. He knows that his time to suffer has come, however, so he makes himself accessible (see 7:6, 30; 8:20; 10:39; 12:23, 27; 13:1; 17:1).

- **What indicates that his opponents thought Jesus would resist?**

They approached him carrying clubs and swords. The other gospel accounts note that Jesus is betrayed with a kiss from Judas; Matthew and Mark explain that it's a prearranged signal so that the officials and soldiers can identify Jesus.

- **How does the group of adversaries react to Jesus? Why?**

When Jesus says, "I am he," they draw back and fall to the ground. D. A. Carson notes that this is probably a natural reaction to the boldness of Jesus in his self-disclosure. Considering that this was probably a large group, this reaction sounds surprising. The *Zondervan NIV Bible Commentary* adds the following observation: "That reply startled the arresting party by its openness and readiness and possibly because it was like the claim he had made previously: 'I am' [see 6:35; 8:12, 58; etc.]. If it were intended as an assertion of deity, his calm demeanor and commanding presence temporarily unnerved his captors."

b. *What is Jesus' concern for his disciples, and how does he show it?*

Recall together that Jesus spoke earlier of protecting his own. Now he is doing just that. Jesus speaks up to identify himself, and he makes clear that he is the one they are seeking. He also says they should let the disciples go.

- **Why does Peter use his sword? What does this tell us about him?**

All of the gospel accounts record Peter drawing his sword, but only John identifies him by name. This incident shows us how frightened and desperate the disciples must have felt (see Luke 22:49). Peter is quick to defend Jesus initially, so he draws his sword, lashes out, and cuts off a servant's ear. Jesus reprimands Peter, and, according to Luke's account, he heals the man's ear. Peter was more than likely surprised by this action and then withdrew from the scene.

c. Why does Jesus say, "Shall I not drink the cup the Father has given me?"

- **What cup is he referring to?**

Jesus is talking about the cup of suffering he will soon face. Figuratively this expression refers to taking on a great burden. Drinking anything makes it a part of you, and Jesus was telling his listeners not to interfere with his determination to lay down his life as the payment for sin.

2. John 18:12-27

a. Where and how is Jesus taken?

- **Do they need to tie Jesus up?**

John reports that Jesus is bound and taken to Annas, the father-in-law of Caiaphas, the high priest. But there's no need to bind Jesus, since he goes along without resistance.

Note: The *NIV Study Bible* includes a helpful note about this hearing: Annas "had been deposed from the high priesthood by the Romans in A.D. 15, but was probably still regarded by many as the true high priest. In Jewish law a man could not be sentenced on the day his trial was held. The two examinations—this one (mentioned only by John) and that before Caiaphas—may have been conducted to give some form of legitimacy to what was done."

b. Who follows Jesus and why?

Peter and another disciple follow Jesus to see what will happen to him. The other disciple, who is known to the high priest, manages to get Peter inside the courtyard to be closer to what's going on.

Note: The unnamed disciple is probably John. Though we can't be certain of his connection to the high priest, we can reasonably guess that his family may have been wealthy or influential enough to have been known to the high priests. Mark 1:19-20 indicates that John's father could afford to hire workers in his fishing business.

c. What happens to Peter in the high priest's courtyard?

The girl at the door challenges him and asks if he is one of Jesus' disciples.

- **Why does Peter deny knowing Jesus?**

Peter is apparently afraid of being arrested along with Jesus.

- Contrast Peter's actions here with the way he acted in the olive grove. Why is he acting cowardly when he was so brave a short time ago?

Peter's bravery appears to have been impulsive, and his denial of Jesus may well be impulsive now. Nonetheless, in this time of testing, Peter shows that his boasting and bravery are not enough to give him the courage to stand up for Jesus. Reflect also on how quickly all of this has happened. Peter has hardly had time to think, and he is known to be rash in decision-making (see John 13:7-9). Peter's actions now seem driven mainly by fear and confusion. Matthew's and Mark's accounts describe him as calling down curses on himself as he attempts to distance himself from Jesus, who is now arrested.

d. *What happens during Jesus' hearing with the high priest?*

The high priest (Annas, according to v. 24) questions Jesus about his teaching and his disciples. He probably wants to have Jesus give his identity and credentials (see again the leaders' interrogation of John the Baptist in 1:19-28). The high priest may also have wanted to know if his disciples were numerous enough to create problems for the trial and sentencing of Jesus. Matthew 26:59 reports that the leaders "were looking for false evidence against Jesus so that they could put him to death."

- **What does Jesus say to defend himself?**

Jesus states that he taught nothing in secret and that any witnesses could testify to this effect. Scholars note that Jewish legal procedure would normally not question the defendant but would ask witnesses to testify.

- **How would you describe Jesus' demeanor or attitude at this point?**

Jesus is fully in charge of his faculties and is not intimidated by the high priest's tactics. Even when he is struck by an official, Jesus points out that there should be some testimony concerning what he had done wrong. At any rate, Annas sends Jesus to be questioned further by the presiding high priest, Caiaphas.

Note: John doesn't include the interview with Caiaphas, but Matthew and Mark do—so you may want to summarize that part of the story briefly or suggest that group members read about it later (see Matt. 26:57-68; Mark 14:53-65). In addition, you may wish to mention that John 18:24 could be translated this way, as stated in an NIV footnote: "(Now Annas had sent him, still bound, to Caiaphas the high priest.)" Regardless of the difficulty of translating the text, however, we can gather that Jesus is tried in a most unusual way—at night, by more than one leading figure, and without reliable witnesses.

    e.   How does Peter respond when he is questioned again?

Peter appears to be alone, and people around the fire are beginning to notice and ask him questions. Other gospel accounts mention that people notice Peter's Galilean accent. A relative of the man whose ear was cut off thinks he recognizes Peter from the arrest in the olive grove. With the spotlight on him again, Peter denies Jesus a second and third time. Then a rooster crows, just as Jesus predicted.

3. John 18:28-32
    a.   Where is Jesus taken next, and why don't the Jewish leaders follow along?

The Jewish leaders take Jesus to the palace of Pilate, the Roman governor. But they do not want to enter the home of this Gentile, because that would make them ceremonially unclean for celebrating the Passover.

    • **What limitation do they have in prosecuting Jesus?**

Under Roman law, the Jewish authorities are not allowed to execute a criminal. As the legal representative of Rome, the governor has to agree with the assessment of capital punishment.

    b.   Discuss the exchange between Pilate and the Jewish leaders.

    • **What seems to be their attitude toward each other?**

Their dialogue indicates mutual dislike and hostility. The Jewish leaders do not want to ask for Pilate's approval, but they have to have it in order to put Jesus to death. Pilate does not want to be bothered by the Jewish leaders or be involved in what is clearly an internal religious matter.

4. John 18:33-40
    a.   Describe the conversation between Pilate and Jesus.

Pilate is curious about Jesus, and Jesus is willing to engage him.

    • **What is Pilate's attitude toward Jesus?**

Though somewhat impatient, Pilate is relatively civil toward Jesus.

- What might indicate that Pilate doesn't know how to respond to Jesus?

Considering the weight of the charges against him, Jesus acted with composure that may have been disarming to Pilate. Matthew and Mark state that Pilate was amazed by Jesus. Jesus even calmly challenges Pilate when he asks if Jesus is a king.

- What is Jesus' attitude toward Pilate?

In verse 37 Jesus clarifies Pilate's earlier question about kingship, and this indicates that Jesus does not write Pilate off but carefully answers his question. As the righteous Son of God, he explains that he has come to bring truth into the world.

- Why do you think Pilate remarks, "What is truth?"

It's difficult to say whether Pilate means this as a philosophical question. He may simply be scornful and fed up with this interrogation thrust upon him in the early morning (18:28). But Pilate may well have been educated with a heavy emphasis on relativism (a common Roman understanding). The fact that he did not wait for an answer from Jesus seems to indicate he did not think there was one. Or perhaps he was afraid to engage Jesus any further.

- How would you respond today to someone who asks, "What is truth?"

b. *What tactics does Pilate use in his attempt to save Jesus from death?*

- What custom does he hope will solve his problem?

Pilate cannot see a reason to condemn Jesus. So, citing a tradition of leniency often granted during the Jewish Passover, he offers to release Jesus. Matthew and Mark report that Pilate knows the religious leaders are trying to kill Jesus out of envy.

- What reaction does Pilate not anticipate?

Pilate does not expect that the Jews will ask instead for the release of Barabbas, a rebel who has been "thrown into prison for insurrection and murder" (Luke 23:25). Normally the Jewish leaders would have nothing to do with zealots who plotted revolts. But in this case they support the release of a dangerous person who can easily put their system of self-rule at risk.

If you have time, you may want to point out that Pilate's wife has had a dream that Jesus is innocent and has told Pilate not to have anything to do with sentencing him (Matt. 27:19). Perhaps this surprising occurrence has also influenced Pilate's hesitation to prosecute Jesus.

Questions for Reflection

If you had been one of Jesus' disciples, how do you think you would have reacted to his arrest and trial? In what ways can you identify with Peter?

In what circumstances can you be bold in identifying with Jesus? In what circumstances are you fearful?

Use these questions both for review and for reflection on circumstances that might make it easy or difficult to stand up for Jesus. Think about whether it's easier to defend Jesus on the spur of the moment or after you've had time to think up a response.

Lesson 10

John 19

"It Is Finished"

Additional Related Scriptures

Exodus 12:46
Leviticus 24:16
Numbers 9:12
Deuteronomy 21:22-23
Psalm 22; 34:20; 69:21
Isaiah 53
Zechariah 12:10

Matthew 26:52-54; 27:27-61
Mark 15:9-10, 15-47
Luke 23:18-56
John 1:29; 3:1-21; 7:45-52; 10:17-18;
    11:45-53
Galatians 3:13
Hebrews 12:2

Introductory Notes

John 19 describes the sentencing, death, and burial of Jesus, "the Lamb of God, who takes away the sin of the world" (John 1:29). Jesus' death is probably the most-studied death in the history of the world, because Christians believe that his death pays the debt of their sin, freeing them to begin new life with God forever. As Romans 6:23 says, "The wages of sin is death, but the gift of God is eternal life in Christ Jesus our Lord." Because Christ laid down his perfect life for our sake, God considers us righteous for his sake. If we believe this good news that the finished work of Christ can save us from eternal death (the penalty of sin), we gain "the right to become children of God" (John 1:12) and have eternal life. As you study this chapter of John, remind yourself that even though Jesus' death was sufficient to save the whole world (John 3:16), his death was also for you personally.

As you prepare to lead, you'll want to review the other gospel accounts to have a full picture of the events covered in this lesson (see Matthew 27:27-61; Mark 15:15-47; Luke 23:18-56). You may also want to recommend that group members later review those passages on their own.

Optional Share Question

Have you ever been accused of something you did not do? How did that make you feel?

1. *John 19:1-11*
   a. *Why do you think Pilate has Jesus flogged?*

   - **Why does Pilate bring Jesus out to the crowd? Does he perhaps think the flogging will satisfy the religious leaders?**

   Luke 23:22 helps us see that Pilate intends at first only to punish Jesus severely and then release him. Pilate apparently thinks this will appease the Jewish leaders' desire to kill Jesus. A person who was flogged was brutally beaten with whips that often had sharp pieces of metal or bone attached at the whipping end. The forty or so lashings deeply lacerated and disfigured the victim's body, often resulting in death. Pilate may well have figured this punishment would be enough to make Jesus a pitiful spectacle and perhaps spare him from execution.

   b. *What's the significance of the soldiers' treatment of Jesus?*

   We can't be certain why the soldiers treated Jesus so cruelly. Perhaps this was a sport to them, and they enjoyed mocking their victims. In many cultures the public spectacle of execution was often treated as entertainment. The soldiers' mockery included a crown of thorns, a purple cloak, verbal insults, spitting, and physical blows. All of these tactics focused on ridiculing Jesus for claiming to be the Jewish Messiah, a king.

   c. *Why is Jesus condemned if Pilate has found no basis for a charge against him?*

   - **Who demands the death penalty for Jesus? Why?**

   Jesus is condemned because at every turn the Jewish leaders have insisted that Pilate execute him. Even though Pilate has found no basis for condemnation, the Jewish leaders use political tactics to prevail over his preference to release Jesus.
   The Jewish leaders are convinced that Jesus has committed blasphemy, because "he claimed to be the Son of God" (John 19:7). But Pilate can tell they have handed Jesus over to him out of envy (Mark 15:9-10). They are afraid that any enhancement of Jesus' standing among the people might cost them their position of leadership and favor with Rome (John 11:48).

   - **Are they right that Jesus claimed to be the Son of God?**

   The Jewish leaders rightly understand that Jesus claimed to be the Son of God, and thus one with God. But they have rejected his claim and want to enforce the law of Moses, which calls for the death penalty in such a case (see Lev. 24:16; John 10:24-39).

d. *How does Jesus respond to Pilate's comment about his power as a Roman governor?*

Jesus points out that Pilate's power has been granted him from above—ultimately from God. Though Pilate may not understand all that Jesus is implying here, Jesus is stating that this interrogation wouldn't be happening if it weren't part of God's plan to save the world from the darkness and slavery of sin.

- **What does Jesus mean by saying that the one who handed him over to Pilate committed the greater sin?**

Jesus is saying that the high priest, representing the leadership of God's people, is responsible for accusing the Son of God of blasphemy, calling for the death penalty, and pushing this matter onto Pilate for a hasty verdict based on envy rather than on righteousness. Though Pilate can't see it, the Righteous One is standing before him, beaten and bloodied, while the guilty party is pointing the finger of accusation from his position of power and favor with Rome. And although Pilate has sinned by going along with the high priest's political games and having Jesus flogged and ridiculed, the greater perpetrator is the religious leader who knows better but has misused his power. (Though some people in your group might think Jesus is referring to Judas here, it was Caiaphas and his close advisors who were responsible for plotting Jesus' death, charging him with blasphemy, and demanding the death penalty from Pilate.)

- **Who, then, is responsible for Jesus' death?**

As we look into the plotting, political intrigue, and individual responsibility of various people involved in the death of Jesus, it's important to remember that God was in control of all this and that it was God's plan to have Jesus die for our sins. From a human point of view, the Jewish religious leaders were responsible for the arrest and ultimate execution of Jesus. Pilate went along with their insistence on the death penalty, and one of Jesus' disciples, Judas Iscariot, betrayed Jesus by leading his enemies to arrest him. But because Jesus, the Word of God, became human in order to die as the Lamb of God for our sins, we have to remember that we all share in the responsibility of his having to come to set us free. And because he laid down his life willingly, we can be thankful and share in the new life he came to give us. The words of an old hymn remind us that he came to die for the sins of each one of us:

Who was the guilty? Who brought this upon you?
It is my treason, Lord, that has undone you.
'Twas I, Lord Jesus, I it was denied you;
I crucified you.

—"Ah, Holy Jesus, How Have You Offended," st. 2;
Psalter Hymnal 386 (CRC Publications, 1987).

2. **John 19:12-16**
   What do the Jewish leaders remind Pilate of in verse 12?

   - **Why do they do this? Does it work?**

   - **Why do you think Pilate gives in to them? What does this tell us about him?**

The religious leaders try to convince Pilate that he will be disloyal to the Roman Caesar if he doesn't execute Jesus for claiming to be a king. "Anyone who claims to be a king opposes Caesar," they add. So Pilate's resolve to try to spare Jesus melts away in the face of political pressure. Here the governor's own moral weakness shows through. Though he's aware that Jesus is innocent, that doesn't really matter to him in the long run. The Jewish leaders' strategy works because Pilate the politician does not want to jeopardize his own standing with Rome.

   - **Whom do the chief priests claim as their king? Are they being sincere?**

The Jewish leaders say they have no king but Caesar, even though they have never really accepted Rome's rule over them. In this way they show they will go to any length to get Pilate to convict Jesus.

Matthew 27:24 notes that Pilate washes his hands in front of the people to symbolize that he is clearing himself of the matter and transferring the responsibility of Jesus' death onto them. But that gesture is as false as the chief priests' claim to recognize Caesar, because the execution could not take place without Pilate's approval.

Note: Though John focuses mainly here on the Jewish leaders' argument that Jesus' claim opposes Caesar, you may wish to note that the other gospel accounts show that Pilate also decides to release Barabbas in Jesus' place, to appease the crowds shouting for Jesus' crucifixion.

3. John 19:17-22

a. Describe the scene of Jesus' crucifixion.

Sentenced to death, Jesus is forced to carry his own cross to a place called Golgotha, which means "the place of the Skull" (see Mark 15:22). The other gospel accounts note that when Jesus is no longer able to carry his own cross, a bystander is ordered to carry it the rest of the way to the crucifixion site. Two criminals are also crucified with Jesus, one on either side of him. Pilate has also ordered that a notice be placed on Jesus' cross, saying, "Jesus of Nazareth, King of the Jews" in three languages: Aramaic, Latin, and Greek.

- **What's the significance of this notice?**

The custom of posting a notice like this informed everyone of the victim's crime. The Romans often crucified criminals along well-traveled roads to remind people who was in charge and how they might be treated if they violated the laws of Rome. The ironic significance of the sign on Jesus' cross is that it proclaimed him king of the Jews, much to the Jewish leaders' dismay. Commentators have also suggested that the message in three languages unwittingly symbolized Jesus' kingship and death for the whole world: Aramaic was the common spoken language of the region, Latin was the official language of Rome, and Greek was the worldwide language of commerce and culture.

- **What is crucifixion?**

Death by crucifixion is usually attributed to the Romans and is often described as one of the cruelest forms of execution. Our word *excruciating*, which refers to intense agony and mind-numbing pain, comes from this practice and literally means "out of the cross." During your discussion it may be eye-opening to explain what crucifixion actually involved. Here's a detailed explanation from a doctor cited in Lee Strobel's book *The Case for Christ*:

> Once a person is hanging in the vertical position, crucifixion is essentially an agonizingly slow death by asphyxiation. The reason is that the stresses on the muscles and diaphragm put the chest into the inhaled position; basically, in order to exhale, the individual must push up on his feet so the tension on the [chest] muscles would be eased for a moment. In doing so, the nail would tear through the foot, eventually locking up against the tarsal bones. After managing to exhale, the person would then be able to relax down and take another breath in. Again he'd have to push himself up to exhale,

scraping his bloodied back against the coarse wood of the cross. This would go on and on until complete exhaustion would take over, and the person wouldn't be able to push up and breathe anymore.

b. What was the significance of Christ's death on a cross?

- **Was Jesus' suffering on the cross only physical?**

Reflect together that at any moment Jesus could have gotten down from the cross and stopped his suffering (see Matt. 26:52-54). Others throughout history have suffered extreme torture, but most, if not all, of them were victims who had no possibility of stopping what was done to them. In addition, Christ suffered the emotional anguish of our sins being placed upon him, and he endured the agony of hell as he paid the penalty for all our sin. We cannot imagine what that was like, but Scripture has described it as enduring the cross and "becoming a curse for us" (Gal. 3:13; see Heb. 12:2). The cross was considered accursed by God and the Jews (see Deut. 21:22-23; Gal. 3:13), and the Romans reserved it for slaves and criminals convicted of the worst of crimes. So the fact that Jesus died on a cross between two criminals illustrated the extent to which he identified with sinners in his death, being "numbered with the transgressors" (Isa. 53:12).

4. *John 19:23-27*

a. What prophecy is fulfilled when the soldiers take Jesus' clothes?

- **What garment are they unable to divide?**

- **Why is this significant?**

Psalm 22:18 prophesies that in the midst of suffering, the Messiah will experience the humiliation of having his clothing divided among his persecutors. John notes, as well, that Jesus' undergarment was seamless, indicating that it was a piece of high-quality clothing. So the soldiers drew lots to decide who would own it. Though David wrote Psalm 22 in the midst of his own suffering, it prefigures in many ways the suffering that Jesus undergoes as the Messiah, "the Son of David" (Matt. 21:9). If you have time during this discussion, you may want to read relevant sections of this psalm to your group.

b. What does Jesus do when he sees his mother standing next to John?

Jesus addresses his mother and his disciple with caring, hopeful words. He turns over his duties as a son to "the disciple whom he loved"—that is, John, the writer of this gospel account (see John 21:23-24). In the midst of overwhelming suffering, Jesus offers encouragement to his mother and gives John the honor of looking after her.

In those days a woman in that culture was totally dependent on a male relative or caretaker, since she could not own property. The *NIV Study Bible* adds, "It may be that Jesus' brothers still did not believe in him (see 7:5)," implying that they were unavailable to care for her—or perhaps would not do so.

- **What's significant about the fact that a group of followers remained with Jesus while he was dying?**

John shows that there is a group of followers who come to be with Jesus during his suffering on the cross. Mary's sister and Mary Magdalene, as well as John, may also be there to comfort Jesus' mother in this time of anguish and grief.

5. *John 19:28-37*

   a. *How do these verses describe the final words of Jesus and the end of his mission?*

John notes that Jesus knows his mission is complete, so he says, "I am thirsty," in order to fulfill Scripture. The *NIV Study Bible* notes that this may refer to Psalm 69:21 and Psalm 22:15. Extreme thirst was a natural consequence of the terrible suffering and exposure Jesus had endured. In addition, his throat may have been so parched that without some liquid he might have been unable to speak. This picture of a weakened, exhausted Christ testifies again to his being fully human as well as fully God (see John 4:6-7). After receiving the drink, Jesus said, "It is finished"—and "with that, he bowed his head and gave up his spirit" (19:30). Note together the emphasis on Jesus' giving up his life rather than having it taken from him (see John 10:17-18).

In addition, the word Jesus uses for "It is finished" means that a complete transaction has taken place. The verb is in the perfect tense, so the single Greek word here (*tetelestai*) means "My work has been fully completed," or "My mission has been totally accomplished," or "My purpose in coming has been fulfilled." In other words, Jesus is saying that his death has paid the price "once for all" for the removal of sin (Heb. 10:10).

   b. *Discuss what occurred next, along with the meaning of the prophecies in verses 36-37.*

- **What do the soldiers do to Jesus?**

- **What do the Scriptures say about this?**

The Jewish leaders do not want the bodies hanging overnight (Deut. 21:23) so they ask Pilate to have the soldiers break the victims' legs. This will hasten their deaths because they won't be able to lift themselves up to breathe.

The gospel notes specifically here that Jesus is already dead. The prophecies in verses 36-37 have to do with Jesus' bones not being broken and his body being pierced. Invite group members to look up the passages cited in the NIV as footnotes to John 19:36-37. Exodus 12:46 and Numbers 9:12 state that the bones of the unblemished lamb prepared for Passover may not be broken. Psalm 34:20 speaks of a righteous man being delivered and protected by God, with not one of his bones being broken. Connecting these passages as references to the Messiah, John is pointing out here that Jesus has been revealed as the Passover Lamb of God, just as John the Baptist had proclaimed at the beginning of Jesus' ministry (John 1:29).

The prophecy in John 19:37 is a direct quote of Zechariah 12:10. Here John uses a key phrase from a passage that applies to the Messiah. The implication is that the Gentiles will "pierce" God in his dwelling place in Jerusalem.

Note: Some group members may have heard that skeptics often doubt whether Jesus was actually dead. A description by a doctor cited in *The Case for Christ* helps to explain:

> Because of what happened when the Roman soldier came around and, being fairly certain that Jesus was dead, confirmed it by thrusting a spear into his right side . . . the spear went through the right lung and into the heart, so when the spear was pulled out, some fluid—the pericardial effusion and the pleural effusion—came out. This would have had the appearance of a clear fluid like water, followed by a large volume of blood, as the eyewitness John described in his gospel. John probably had no idea why he saw both blood and a clear fluid come out. . . . Yet John's description is consistent with what modern medicine would expect to have happened. . . . There is absolutely no doubt that Jesus was dead.

6. *John 19:38-42*

   What's the significance of Jesus' burial place and the role of Joseph and Nicodemus in burying Jesus' body?

Knowing that Jesus' body must be removed and buried before the Sabbath begins, a secret disciple named Joseph, cited in Luke 23:50 as a member of the Jewish ruling council, steps forward with Nicodemus, another council member (John 3:1), to take care of these matters. They apparently see the importance of providing a proper burial place for Jesus' body. Since Jesus has been executed as a criminal, he would otherwise likely be buried in a common grave outside the city. Even his family cannot claim his body, but Joseph has social standing, and he can approach Pilate to ask for Jesus' body.

John notes that the tomb where Joseph places Jesus' body is in a garden near the place where Jesus has been crucified, and in Matthew's account we learn that this is Joseph's "own new tomb that he had cut out of the rock" (Matt. 27:60). Scholars have also noted that the use of this tomb for Jesus' body would have excluded its use for anyone in Joseph's family, since individuals from different families were not customarily buried in the same place.

- **What does this tell us about Joseph?**

At the very least, Joseph was willing to give up something costly for the sake of Jesus. And although he has been only a secret disciple of Jesus, he is now bold enough (see Mark 15:43) to step forward and show respect for Jesus, at least in terms of giving the Messiah a decent burial.

- **Why do you think Nicodemus stepped forward at this time?**

As we've noted in earlier lessons, Nicodemus has been drawn to Jesus' teaching for some time (John 3:1-21). He even spoke up to question the Pharisees' hasty assumptions about Jesus during the Feast of Tabernacles (7:45-52). Apparently by this time, like Joseph, he was ready to step forward and at least help provide a decent burial for Jesus.

Note: The seventy-five pounds of myrrh and aloes would have been very expensive. Commentators note that this amount could almost be called excessive. Custom called for wrapping the body with strips of linen (like bandages) and putting the spices inside. Joseph and Nicodemus would have had to do all this quickly to finish their "work" before the Sabbath began.

Question for Reflection

As an exercise that can help you tell this story to someone who hasn't heard it before, imagine yourself to be one of the individuals present at Jesus' crucifixion and describe what you would have seen and experienced and how you might have felt.

Lesson 11

John 20

Risen from the Dead!

Additional Related Scriptures

Matthew 28	Romans 3:21-5:5; 10:17
Mark 16	1 Corinthians 15:42-49
Luke 23:54; 24:1-49	2 Corinthians 5:17-21
John 11:16, 25-26; 19:42	Philippians 3:20-21
Acts 1-2	Hebrews 11:1, 7-28

Introductory Notes

When he spoke with Mary of Bethany as she grieved the death of her brother, Jesus said, "I am the resurrection and the life. He who believes in me will live, even though he dies; and whoever lives and believes in me will never die" (John 11:25-26). The account of Jesus' own resurrection in John 20 shows that this was no empty promise. Because Jesus came back to life, we have the living hope that we too, even if we die, will live again someday— and that our life in him begins even now (John 20:31; 2 Cor. 5:17; Phil. 3:20; 1 Pet. 1:3-9).

Before discussing this lesson with your group, you may wish to note that there seem to be a few discrepancies between the gospel accounts on Jesus' resurrection. Some group members may be aware of these differences in details and have questions about them. As we have noted earlier, this doesn't mean the Bible contains "mistakes." We need to be aware that seamless harmony among their accounts and accuracy of detail weren't as important to the original writers as we might prefer today. We can still share in the good news of these accounts as we accept their central message by faith. (See additional comments in lesson 2 under question 1b.)

Optional Share Question

Discuss a time when someone told you something that sounded impossible but that turned out to be real or true. Explain how you felt.

1. *John 20:1-9*

Note: Mary Magdalene has often become a figure of interest in religious history, and renewed intrigue about her life and character has surfaced again recently. Most of the hype, however, is fictional. What we know from the Bible is that Mary Magdalene was a woman whom Jesus healed of demon possession and who became one of his followers (Mark 16:9; Luke

8:1-3). She even helped to support Jesus' ministry out of her own financial resources (Luke 8:2-3). Some people have thought she was the woman in John 8 who was caught in adultery, and some have speculated that she was the "woman who had lived a sinful life" and interrupted a party to wash Jesus' feet (Luke 7:36-50). Though some movies have portrayed her that way, Scripture does not support that perspective. Further, nothing in Scripture indicates a romantic connection between Mary Magdalene and Jesus, as some dramatizations and novels have suggested.

Probably the most significant (though often overlooked) fact about Mary Magdalene is that, according to the Bible, she was the first person to whom Jesus appeared after his resurrection (Mark 16:9; John 20:1, 10-16) and with whom he entrusted the good news that he had risen (20:17-18). Another significant fact is that she and other women are mentioned consistently and prominently as witnesses to the resurrection. These facts actually help to testify to the truth of Jesus' resurrection. Considering that women were not perceived as reliable witnesses in Jesus' day (for example, they could not testify in a court of law), scholars have noted that if anyone in those days had wanted to fabricate the story of Jesus' resurrection, they would not have claimed women as the first witnesses.

a.   When did Mary go to the tomb, and what did she discover there?

- **Why was she at the tomb so early?**

- **What did she think had happened?**

Mary Magdalene went to the tomb before sunrise on the first day of the week—that is, Sunday. As the accounts in Mark and Luke suggest, she had gone there to anoint Jesus' body again with burial spices or ointment. Recall that Joseph and Nicodemus had hastily buried the body and wrapped it with spices on Friday afternoon just before the special Sabbath of Passover (Luke 23:54; John 19:42). During the Sabbath, which began at sunset on Friday and lasted throughout Saturday, no Jew would have been allowed to visit the tomb.

So the first opportunity for Mary to visit the tomb was when she woke on Sunday morning before dawn. When she arrived at the tomb, however, Mary saw that the stone that should have sealed the tomb "had been removed" (John 20:1).

Understandably upset, she ran to find Peter and John ("the other disciple") and said, "They have taken the Lord out of the tomb . . . !" (20:2). From the text it seems she did not look into the tomb but thought immediately that Jesus' body was stolen.

Commentator D. A. Carson reports that grave robbing was rather common in that day. Around the same time period, Emperor Claudius of

Rome ordered that "destroying tombs, removing bodies, or even displacing the sealing stones," was a crime punishable by death. Apparently bodies were commonly stolen for the expensive linen and spices in which they were wrapped.

    b. How did Peter and John respond when Mary spoke to them?

- **What did they see, and how did they react?**

Peter and John rushed to the tomb. John, who arrived first, looked into the tomb from outside and saw the linen strips that had wrapped Jesus' body earlier. When Peter arrived, he went into the tomb and saw the linen strips as well as "the burial cloth that had been around Jesus' head. The cloth was folded up . . . separate from the linen" (20:7). Then John went inside "and believed."

- **What does it mean that John believed?**

- **What does the text say about the disciples' understanding?**

The *NIV Study Bible* notes, "John did not say what he believed, but it must have been that Jesus was resurrected." And regarding the comment in verse 9, it says, "First they came to know of the resurrection through what they saw in the tomb; only later did they see it in Scripture. It is obvious they did not make up a story of resurrection to fit a preconceived understanding of Scriptural prophecy."

Noting that "a specific knowledge . . . of a specific portion of Scripture" would be required here—"presumably Ps. 16:10"—*The New Bible Commentary* adds, "It is deeply ingrained in gospel records that understanding did not come even to the disciples until after the resurrection, and even then only gradually."

2. *John 20:10-18*
    a. What occurred when Mary remained at the tomb?

- **What did she see?**

- **What did the angels ask Mary?**

As she wept, Mary looked inside the tomb and saw two angels sitting where Jesus' body had been. They asked her why she was crying, and she said, just as she had told Peter and John, "They have taken my Lord away . . . and I don't know where they have put him" (John 20:13). The possibility of resurrection must not have occurred to her at that point.

b.   What happened when Mary turned around?

- **Who was the person behind her?**

After speaking to the angels, which must have been a shocking experience in itself, Mary realized someone was behind her. When she turned around, this person also asked why she was crying and added, "Who is it you are looking for?" (20:15). At first Mary thought this was the gardener, so she asked him to tell her where the body was, if he knew. But when she heard the man speak her name, she knew it was Jesus.

- **Why didn't Mary recognize Jesus right away?**

The text doesn't state why Mary didn't know right away that this was Jesus. In some of Jesus' other post-resurrection appearances, his followers didn't recognize him at first either (Luke 24:15-16, 37; John 21:4). Though we can't be certain, the reason may be as simple as not being able to see clearly in the semi-darkness before sunrise, especially with tears in her eyes. Or perhaps Jesus looked different, as suggested in the later-manuscript addition at the end of Mark's gospel (Mark 16:12).

- **What evidence of faith do we see here?**

Mary suddenly understood that Jesus was not dead but alive. The best evidence of her faith is her response: "Rabboni!"—a more familiar address than "Rabbi" (commentators note that "My Teacher!" is a closer translation than the one John gives in verse 16).

- **Why didn't Jesus want Mary to hold on to him?**

The text here is difficult to understand, but apparently Jesus was referring to his ascension—and perhaps to having a different kind of body (see John 20:19, 26; 1 Cor. 15:42-49). Though his ascension had not yet occurred, it called for a new kind of relationship between Jesus and his disciples—a relationship through the Holy Spirit (see John 16:5-16).

- **What did he tell her to do?**

Jesus told Mary to go and tell his "brothers"—the disciples—that he was returning to God the Father.

- **What comfort did his words offer?**

The address "brothers" implied a personal relationship, suggesting the closeness of members of the same family. In addition, the reference to "my Father and your Father . . . my God and your God" suggested a familiar, personal relationship shared by the Father, Jesus, and his followers.

3. John 20:19-23

   a. Describe what happened when Jesus appeared to the disciples.

   - **How did they react to Jesus' presence?**

   - **What did he say to them?**

The disciples had gathered in a locked room because they feared being arrested by the authorities. Suddenly Jesus appeared in their midst, even though the doors were locked, and greeted them with the words "Peace be with you!" Then he showed them his hands and side so they could see that it was really him.

Luke's account says the disciples thought at first that he was a ghost, so Jesus asked for some food and ate it to show that he had a physical body (Luke 24:26-43). If questions arise about Jesus' resurrected body and whether it reveals anything about the resurrection bodies believers can look forward to, refer group members to 1 Corinthians 15:42-49 and Philippians 3:20-21.

   b. What additional words of encouragement did Jesus give the disciples?

Again Jesus spoke the comforting phrase, "Peace be with you." Certainly this was more than a greeting; it was a promise that encouraged the disciples to rest in the peace of God available to them in Jesus' presence. This would also be available later through the presence of the Holy Spirit.

Jesus also reminded the disciples that in the same sense that the Father had sent him, he was now sending them into the world to spread the good news of salvation. In this way Jesus showed that he was restoring them to their position of being disciples and messengers of God.

   - **What did Jesus mean in verses 22-23?**

We might wonder if when he said, "Receive the Holy Spirit" (20:22), Jesus was pouring out the Spirit on his disciples at this time rather than on Pentecost (fifty days after Passover). But at this point it appears he was giving a promise that would be fulfilled on Pentecost. It's evident from the disciples' actions that the Spirit did not come upon them in power and transform them to be Christ's messengers until Pentecost (see John 21; Acts 1-2).

Regarding verse 23, the *NIV Study Bible* explains, "God does not forgive people's sins because we do so, nor does he withhold forgiveness because we do. Rather, those who proclaim the gospel are in effect forgiving or not forgiving sins, depending on whether the hearers accept or reject Jesus Christ."

4. John 20:24-29

    a. Give a character sketch of Thomas.

Group members may come up with a number of comments about Thomas having little faith. But it's important to remember that Thomas earlier showed enough courage to say that the disciples should all go with Jesus to Jerusalem and die with him (John 11:16). Because of this episode in John 20, Thomas is often referred to as "Doubting Thomas," but we should also note that he confesses Jesus with confidence when he is inspired with courage in Jesus' presence.

    b. Can you identify in any way with how Thomas felt? Why or why not?

Many people can identify with Thomas's position. Thomas simply did not trust the testimony of the disciples; he wanted more evidence than they could offer. Invite group members to reflect and share their thoughts, if they wish, on whether faith and trust come easy to them.

- **How did Jesus respond to Thomas, and why?**

Jesus responded in a way that seems he had heard Thomas's statement of unbelief even before he appeared in the locked room. In fact, Jesus used Thomas's very words. Knowing of Thomas's devotion, the Lord now wanted to bring this disciple's imperfect faith to fruition. He challenged Thomas to see his wounds and touch them. Then he told Thomas to "stop doubting and believe" (21:27).

    c. How did Thomas respond to Jesus?

Thomas responded with one of the greatest biblical statements affirming the deity of Jesus. Note together that this is also the Bible's first post-resurrection confession of Jesus as Lord and God. The Thomas who doubted was surely a believer now.

d. *What did Jesus say about others who will believe?*

- **What does this mean?**

- **Who are these believers?**

Jesus said that others who believe without seeing him will be blessed. These believers are all who have had true faith in God from even before the time of Jesus until today—and beyond. As Hebrews 11:1 states, "Faith is being sure of what we hope for and certain of what we do not see." People from ancient times, such as Noah, Abraham and Sarah, Moses and his parents, and many others had such belief and faith, and God credited it to them as righteousness on the basis of the sacrifice Jesus would make (John 1:29; Rom. 3:21-5:5; Heb. 11:7-28). In addition, all people who have believed in Jesus since he came are also credited with his righteousness. (See also Rom. 10:17; 2 Cor. 5:7, 17-21.)

5. *John 20:30-31*
   a. *What information does John add in these verses?*

John notes that his gospel account is only a partial account of what Jesus actually did. He makes clear that Jesus did many other miraculous signs in the presence of his disciples.

   b. *Why has John written this book?*

John says he has written this account to encourage people to believe that Jesus is the Christ (Messiah), the Son of God, and that by believing they may have eternal life. In other words, John's gospel account is not simply a volume of information. It calls for a response of faith.

Question for Reflection
   What's your response to this book John has written? How would you describe it to others?

Lesson 12
John 21

"Follow Me!"

Additional Related Scriptures

Matthew 26:33-34; 28:10
Mark 16:7
Luke 5:1-11

John 6:1-15; 10:11, 14-16; 12:27-28;
13:37-38; 15:8, 18-21; 16:7-16;
17:13-26; 18:17, 25-27
Galatians 2:11-13
1 Peter 1:1-9; 5:1-4

Introductory Notes

On the Sea of Tiberias (Sea of Galilee) after a long night of fishing without a catch, a group of Jesus' disciples are returning to shore in the early morning. There's a man on shore whom they fail to recognize at first. The man is Jesus, and he still has some things to teach his disciples. In this closing chapter of John's gospel account, Jesus again teaches as clearly with his actions as with his words. And he provides an amazing model for relational ministry, servant leadership, and forgiveness.

Optional Share Question

Think of a time when you were given another chance at an important task you had failed to do. Describe how you felt about failing and how you felt about receiving another chance. How did things turn out?

1. *John 21:1-6*

   a. *Who's been out fishing, and what has gone wrong?*

   • **Why do you think they're fishing?**

At the Sea of Tiberias (Sea of Galilee) the apostle Peter, who made his living as a fisherman before meeting Jesus, has said, "I'm going fishing," and a group of disciples with him have said, "We'll go with you." After a whole night out on the lake, however, they've caught nothing.

Commentators and other scholars are divided on whether this is an act of defiance (going back to old ways) or simply a practical use of time while the disciples wait for more instruction from Jesus. It's likely that they're in Galilee because Jesus has sent word to meet him there (Matt. 28:10; Mark 16:7). But we're not told how much time has passed since Jesus rose from the grave.

b. *Who is standing on shore, and what does he tell them?*

Jesus is on shore as the disciples are out fishing, but they don't recognize him.

- **What does he say to them?**

Jesus asks if they have caught any fish, and when they tell him they haven't caught any, he tells them to throw their net on the right side of the boat.

- **What happens then?**

When they cast their net on the right side, they catch so many fish that they cannot haul the net into the boat.

- **Why do you think they did as he said?**

Perhaps they were eager for advice after catching nothing all night, or perhaps Jesus' manner conveyed guidance and help in a way that inspired them. (After all, this was the Lord who was guiding them.) Again, as in Luke 5:5, Jesus is helping his disciples to catch fish. In the previous instance of a miraculous catch of fish, Jesus connected it to fishing for people. Soon they would be doing that fulltime. Take a few moments to compare this fishing experience with the one in Luke 5:1-11.

2. *John 21:7-14*

a. *Who recognizes the Lord, and what does Peter do in response?*

John says, "It is the Lord!" And as soon as Peter hears John say this, he springs into action.

- **How is this action consistent with Peter's character as we have seen it?**

Commentator Leon Morris has observed, "Peter generally acts before John does, and John generally understands before Peter does." One is perceptive, and the other is an activist.

b.   What's significant about the abundant catch of fish?

- **Why do you think the actual number of fish is given?**

People have tried to read meaning into the exact number of fish. Even though numbers often have significance in Scripture, that simply may not be the case with this number. The *Zondervan NIV Bible Commentary* notes that "the exact number of fish and the fact that the net did not break reflect both an eyewitness account and a fisherman's perspective." Probably most significant is that this miraculous catch is a reminder of Jesus' original call to his disciples.

c.   When the disciples reach shore, what do they see?

- **What does this tell us about Jesus?**

- **Why has he cooked them breakfast?**

- **What can we learn from this?**

Spend some time discussing the significance of this humble act. Jesus has taken the time to build a fire and prepare food for the disciples. On the night before his death, he washed their feet; now he prepares food for them. Again he models what servant leadership is all about. No job is too menial. Jesus, the Word who was with God at creation (John 1:1-2), the One who made all the varieties of fish in the sea and designed the physical properties that result in burning coals, is now cooking breakfast for his friends! As always, Jesus serves as the supreme example for his disciples, and he prepares them to take up God's mission in the world by following him.

- **Can we ever say that Jesus does not care about our daily needs?**

- **What does this show us about how we should serve others?**

- **Do you think Jesus wanted to remind the disciples of an earlier incident in which he provided food?**

Recall the feeding of many thousands in which Jesus multiplied a few fish and some barley loaves (John 6:1-15).

- **How might this gesture give the disciples comfort?**

They could be assured that their daily needs would be met in their future with Jesus.

3. *John 21:15-17*

   a. *What does Jesus ask Peter after they have finished eating?*

The question Jesus poses is "Do you truly love me more than these?"

• **What does Jesus mean by the words "more than these"?**

The *NIV Study Bible* notes that this phrase "may mean 'more than you love these men' or 'more than these men love me' or 'more than you love these things' (i.e., the fishing gear). Perhaps the second [possibility] is best, for Peter had claimed a devotion above that of the others" just before Jesus had said Peter would deny him three times (see Matt. 26:33-34; John 13:37-38).

• **Why does he ask him this question three times?**

Most scholars believe that Jesus does this because Peter denied knowing Jesus three times on the night of his arrest (John 18:17, 25-27).
Joseph Ryan expresses the situation this way, "Jesus asks Peter if he is still struggling for control. Peter, the man of action, knows how to live his life only if he is in control; and Jesus tells him he can't be in control. . . . *Do you love me, Simon?* is a question that cuts through all of Peter's pretension and [his] attempts to control. It cuts to the heart of the failure in his denial of Christ."

• **How does this inquiry make Peter feel?**

Peter is hurt that Jesus asks him this question three times (21:17), likely reminding him of his three-time failure to live up to his boastful promises.

   b. *In response to Peter's answers, what does Jesus tell Peter to do?*

• **How is Jesus giving Peter another chance to serve faithfully?**

After each response, Jesus tells Peter to take care of his sheep. Coming from the good shepherd, who laid down his life for his sheep (John 10:11, 14-16), this statement shows that Jesus is entrusting Peter with a responsibility dear to his heart. Jesus is now asking the fisherman to become a shepherd with all that this work of servant leadership involves. He is commissioning Peter to take care of the flock (people) that God will entrust to him.
In 1 Peter 1:1-5, written by Peter when he was an older man, we find that he did what Jesus asked. No longer the brash fisherman, Peter knew that to be used by God, he needed to be humbled and dependent on "the Chief Shepherd" (see 1 Pet. 5:1-4).

4. John 21:18-19

a. What prediction does Jesus make about Peter?

- **Why does Jesus say this?**

As John explains in verse 19, Jesus tells Peter about the manner of death he will have to face. Jesus draws attention to the importance of this statement by introducing it with the words, "I tell you the truth." Its connection with the commission "Feed my sheep" implies that it follows or results from Peter's obedience to this command. In other words, if Peter follows the command to feed the Lord's sheep, he can expect to live long enough to accomplish this task, but in the end he will, like Jesus, be called upon to sacrifice his life. Jesus' words here appear to suggest crucifixion, considering the idea of stretching out one's hands. Whatever the case, it will be a death that will be forced upon him.

Commentator F. F. Bruce points out that by the time of the writing of John's gospel account, Peter was likely already martyred, having followed Jesus not only in life but also in death.

- **Why would this death "glorify" God?**

Just as Jesus often taught that his own mission and death would bring glory to God, so his followers who served and died for the sake of the Savior would glorify God (John 12:27-28; 15:8, 18-21; 16:13-14; 17:13-26).

b. What's the significance of Jesus' saying, "Follow me!"

- **When had Jesus given this command earlier?**

With this closing word in his discussion about shepherding his flock, Jesus offers encouragement and opens the door to a new chapter in God's mission. Jesus is reinstating Peter with the challenge and invitation he used at the very beginning of his ministry, when he first met Peter on the shore of Galilee and said, "Follow me . . ." (Matt. 4:19). In Jesus' use of this command, we can see that the Lord has been leading up to this moment by meeting his disciples on the shore, supplying a miraculous catch of fish, serving them food, addressing Peter's failure, and calling this disciple, as well as all the others, to service again.

5. John 21:20-23

What distracts Peter next, and how does Jesus respond?

- **Why do you think Peter is interested in what will happen to the other disciple?**

When Peter has heard Jesus' words of commission and reinstatement, he notices another disciple—John—following them as they walk along the shore. And he now wants to know what John's future will be.

Peter's question is probably motivated mainly by curiosity, but it shows that he is still easily distracted from the mission Jesus is calling him to. Neither he nor any of the other disciples will be fully equipped for this mission until the Spirit comes at Pentecost (Acts 2; see John 16:7-15). Even after that point they will make mistakes (see Gal. 2:11-13), but the Lord will continue to work through them, just as he does with us today.

Jesus responds with a gentle reminder that this is none of Peter's business. The length of John's life and service is up to the Lord and should not be Peter's concern.

- **What lesson can we learn from this admonition?**

- **What clarification is made in verse 23?**

John notes that a rumor developed because of Jesus' statement "If I want him to remain alive until I return, what is that to you?" Some people falsely assumed that this meant John would never die. So John makes clear that this statement doesn't mean he won't die.

6. *John 21:24-25*
What does John want to communicate as he closes this book?

The point of this closing statement is to confirm that John has written a truthful testimony of Jesus' life and teaching. With the words "This is the disciple who testifies . . ." this verse also confirms that the identity of the unnamed disciple throughout this gospel account is John himself.

- **Why are the words "we" and "his" used in verse 24?**

Many commentators see this statement as an insertion by a scribe or copyist who wants to verify John's testimony for a later generation of believers who have not witnessed the events in this book or heard them firsthand from an eyewitness. A similar concern about eyewitness testimony is apparent in John's first letter to believers facing the challenges of Christian living in this world (1 John 1:1-4).

Other scholars such as D. A. Carson favor the idea that John is using the literary "we" as found in John 1:14: "We have seen his glory."

- **What do you think is the main message of verse 25?**

Jesus undoubtedly did many other things. Even with the other gospel accounts we do not have a complete record of everything Jesus did. What we do have is sufficient to show us what Jesus came to accomplish for us. John is saying that Jesus did amazing things, but the key to understanding all this is the truth Jesus stated in John 3:16, "God so loved the world that he gave his one and only Son, that whoever believes in him shall not perish but have eternal life." Joseph Ryan comments, "As a truthful and passionate witness to the events and meaning of Christ's life, death, and resurrection, [John] calls on his readers to respond with like passion and love for the truth. John is not neutral about Jesus Christ."

- **Can the same be said about us?**

Questions for Reflection

How has your life been affected by studying the eyewitness account of Jesus as written by John?

In what ways has this study helped to prepare you to spread the good news to others?

Are you called to tend the flock and feed the sheep of the good shepherd? Explain.

Be sensitive to Jesus' working in the hearts of your group members. Though some may hesitate to speak openly about following Jesus and putting their full trust in him, they may speak more freely if you take the lead. You can do that by affirming that Jesus, the Son of God, the Word of God, became a human being like us to save us from sin and give us eternal life. For our sake he became the Lamb of God, dying to pay for our sin, and he rose again so that we can have new life with God forever. As our Chief Shepherd who rules in heaven over all things today, Jesus guides us faithfully to serve God by the power of the Holy Spirit—all to the glory of God.

For anyone who may be ready to make or renew a commitment to Jesus as Lord and Savior, see "An Invitation" and "Prayer of Commitment" at the back of the study guide and on the next page of this leader guide.

An Invitation

Listen now to what God is saying to you.

You may be aware of things in your life that keep you from coming near to God. You may have thought of God as someone who is unsympathetic, angry, and punishing. You may feel as if you don't know how to pray or how to come near to God.

"But because of his great love for us, God, who is rich in mercy, made us alive with Christ even when we were dead in transgressions—it is by grace you have been saved" (Eph. 2:4-5). Jesus, God's Son, died on the cross to save us from our sins. It doesn't matter where you come from, what you've done in the past, or what your heritage is. God has been watching over you and caring for you, drawing you closer. "You also were included in Christ when you heard the word of truth, the gospel of your salvation" (Eph. 1:13).

Do you want to receive Jesus as your Savior and Lord? It's as simple as A-B-C:

- Admit that you have sinned and that you need God's forgiveness.
- Believe that God loves you and that Jesus has already paid the price for your sins.
- Commit your life to God in prayer, asking the Lord to forgive your sins, nurture you as his child, and fill you with the Holy Spirit.

Prayer of Commitment

Here is a prayer of commitment recognizing Jesus Christ as Savior. If you long to be in a loving relationship with Jesus, pray this prayer. If you have already committed your life to Jesus, use this prayer for renewal and praise.

Dear God, I come to you simply and honestly to confess that I have sinned, that sin is a part of who I am. And yet I know that you listen to sinners who are truthful before you. So I come with empty hands and heart, asking for forgiveness.

I confess that only through faith in Jesus Christ can I come to you. I confess my need for a Savior, and I thank you, Jesus, for dying on the cross to pay the price for my sins. Father, I ask that you forgive my sins and count me as righteous for Jesus' sake. Remove the guilt that accompanies my sin and bring me into your presence.

Holy Spirit of God, help me to pray, and teach me to live by your Word. Faithful God, help me to serve you faithfully. Make me more like Jesus each day, and help me to share with others the good news of your great salvation. In Jesus' name, Amen.

Bibliography

It is our hope that you will have opportunities to encourage members of your group who may be starting their spiritual journey. This bibliography includes some works that aim to help people who may be skeptical about Jesus or who have had little or no exposure to Christianity. Resources like these can help you "give an answer . . . with gentleness and respect" (1 Pet. 3:15).

Barker, Kenneth L., and John R. Kohlenberger III. *Zondervan NIV Bible Commentary.* Grand Rapids, Mich.: Zondervan, 1994.

Boice, James M. *The Gospel of John.* Grand Rapids, Mich.: Baker, 2001.

Bowen, John P. *Evangelism for "Normal" People.* Minneapolis: Augsburg, 2002.

Bruce. F. F. *The Gospel of John.* Grand Rapids, Mich.: Eerdmans, 2004.

Carson, D. A. *The Gospel According to John.* Grand Rapids, Mich.: Eerdmans, 1991.

Guthrie, D., and J. A. Motyer, eds. *The New Bible Commentary: Revised.* Grand Rapids, Mich.: Eerdmans, 1970.

Morris, Leon. *The Gospel of John.* Grand Rapids, Mich.: Eerdmans, 1975.

NIV Serendipity Bible for Study Groups. Grand Rapids, Mich.: Zondervan, 1989.

NIV Study Bible. Grand Rapids, Mich.: Zondervan, 1985.

Ryan, Joseph. *That You May Believe.* Wheaton, Ill.: Crossway, 2003.

Strobel, Lee. *The Case for Christ.* Grand Rapids, Mich.: Zondervan, 1998.

Tasker, R. V. G. *The Gospel According to John.* Grand Rapids, Mich.: Eerdmans, 1971.

Yancey, Philip. *Where Is God When It Hurts?* Grand Rapids, Mich.: Zondervan, 1997.

Zacharias, Ravi. *Jesus Among Other Gods.* Nashville: Thomas Nelson, 2000.

Evaluation Questionnaire

DISCOVER JOHN: THE LAMB OF GOD

As you complete this study, please fill out this questionnaire to help us evaluate the effectiveness of our materials. Please be candid. Thank you.

1. Was this a home group ___ or a church-based ___ program? What church?

2. Was the study used for
   ___ a community evangelism group?
   ___ a community faith-nurture group?
   ___ a church Bible study group?

3. How would you rate the materials?

   Study Guide
   ___ excellent ___ very good ___ good ___ fair ___ poor

   Leader Guide
   ___ excellent ___ very good ___ good ___ fair ___ poor

4. What were the strengths?

5. What were the weaknesses?

6. What would you suggest to improve the material?

7. In general, what was the experience of your group?

Your name (optional) _____

Address _____

8. Other comments:

(Please fold, tape, stamp, and mail. Thank you.)

Faith Alive Christian Resources
2850 Kalamazoo Ave. SE
Grand Rapids, MI 49560